A CIP catalogue of this book is available from the National Library of Australia.
Messenger, Lisa
Purpose: Find Your Why and the How Will Look After Itself
ISBN 9 780995 35 2636
First published in 2017 by The Messenger Group Pty Ltd
PO Box H241
Australia Square NSW 1215

Editing: Amy Molloy, Jen Taylor and Sarah Megginson
Proofreader: Jen Taylor
Production Manager: Ashleigh Hipwood
Book design: Tess Maguire, No Agency
Cover design: Emily Ponton
Illustrations: 'The Doers' by Jen and Jennifer (page 62–65), 'The Dream' by Natasha Saba, The Curly Collective (page 84)
Photography of Lisa: Scott Ehler
Hair and make-up: Jessica Diez, oneninetynine management
Styling of Lisa: Jeff Lack
Clothing: Mother Of Pearl Madeline Rose Heart Print Blouse from Parlour X, Jacquemus Ruffle Skirt Red from Parlour X, Ginger & Smart Euphoria Tie Sandals, Samantha Wills Bohemian Bardot Ring (cover), Rolla's Eastcoast Ankle Jean, Neuw Denim Studio Crew Sweater, Carvela Nude Stud Heels by Kurt Geiger (page 71), Proenza Schouler Ostrich Feather Pencil Skirt from Parlour X, Neuw Denim Leather Biker Jacket, Carvela Navy Stud Heels by Kurt Geiger (page 196), Christopher Esber Stellastella Off Shoulder Top from Parlour X, Country Road shorts – Lisa's own, Ginger & Smart Euphoria Tie Sandals (page 205)
Distribution enquiries: Claire Belbeck, claire@collectivehub.com

This is proudly a Collective product
collectivehub.com

DISCLAIMER
The content of this book is to serve as a general overview of matters of interest and is not intended to be comprehensive, nor does it constitute financial (or other) advice in any way. This book is a compilation of one person's ideas, concepts, ideologies, philosophies and opinions. You should carry out your own research and/or seek your own professional advice before acting or relying on any of the information displayed in this book. The author, Messenger Group Pty Ltd and its related entities will not be liable for any loss or damage (financial or otherwise) that may arise out of your improper use of, or reliance on, the content of this book. You accept sole responsibility of the outcomes if you choose to adopt and/or use the ideas, concepts, ideologies, philosophies and opinions within the content of this book.

PURPOSE

Find Your Why And The
How Will Look After Itself

TO MY TEAM

THE BEAUTIFUL INDIVIDUALS WHO MAKE UP COLLECTIVE HUB

WE'RE IN THIS DREAM TOGETHER IN OUR SHARED PURPOSE TO IGNITE HUMAN POTENTIAL.

I BELIEVE IN OUR VISION.
LET'S NOT STOP HERE.

AND TO THE COLLECTIVE HUB COMMUNITY,
YOU ARE THE ONES WHO KEEP ME ON PURPOSE
AND INSPIRE ME TO KEEP GOING
- EVEN ON THE TOUGHEST DAYS.

I HOPE THIS BOOK OF MY OWN PERSONAL JOURNEY MIGHT HELP YOU STEP INTO YOURS

x Lisa

We make countless decisions every day about what we'll do with our time and energy.

We think through logistics, juggle commitments, prioritise and evaluate.

But... do we stop long enough to consider why we are doing it?

..What an absolute
tragedy, when almost
everything in life stems
from your why.

**AND WE KNOW
FRIEDRICH NIETZSCHE'S
SENTIMENT TO BE TRUE:**

*If we have our own Why in life,
we shall get along with almost any How.*

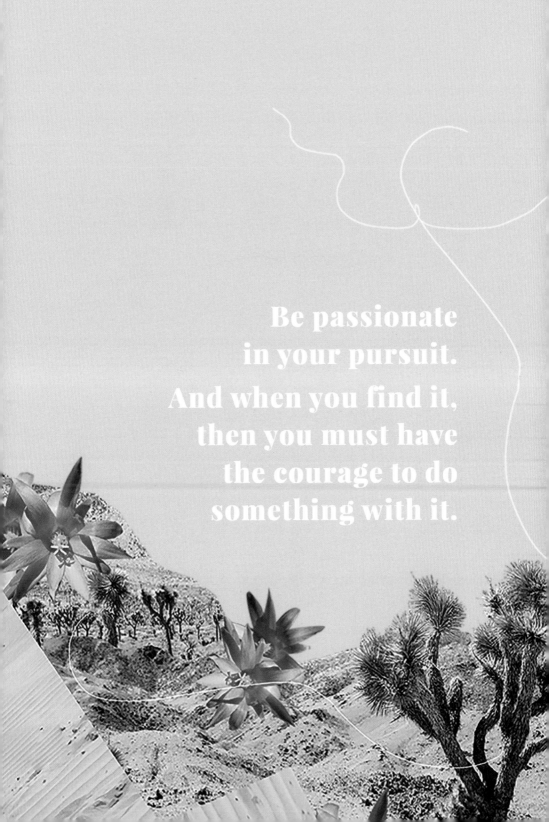

Be passionate
in your pursuit.
And when you find it,
then you must have
the courage to do
something with it.

The two most important days in your life are the day you were born and the day you find out why.

Why?

MAKE IT YOUR
ULTIMATE, DEFINITIVE,
ALL-CONSUMING,
LIFE-ALTERING
(QUESTION TO SEEK.

Contents

Introduction

Why do you go to work every day… really? Why do you open your eyes and, instead of deciding to sit on the couch for the next eight hours, decide to move yourself, challenge yourself, *give* yourself and, sometimes, sacrifice yourself… day after day, week after week, year after year – for a lifetime?

How do you feel at the end of a workday? As you close down your computer, say goodbye to your last customer or tell your colleague you'll see them in the morning, how do you feel in your heart, in your mind, in your body? Relieved it's over? Excited for tomorrow? Exhausted, downtrodden, uplifted, grateful, hopeful, frustrated or content?

Have you ever woken up an hour before your alarm clock was due to go off, so excited to begin your workday that you *chose* to get up before sunrise to get started? No? Well, that could be because you haven't discovered your Why yet – that vital reason, that amazing feeling, that magic sentence that makes every day of your life make sense.

I do this ——————————————

because I hope to ——————————————

For the last five years, I feel I have been completely, absolutely and unquestionably on purpose. It makes me glow to be able to say that! Being in flow and 100 per cent living my passion and my Why, I have woken up every single day knowing exactly what drives me. But, it wasn't always that way. And I know from meeting and speaking to thousands of people every week at conferences, events and across all of our digital and social platforms, that a lot of you are still searching for the illusive Why in your lives. I'm here to help you find it.

You may know the story of *Collective Hub* by now – the disruptive magazine platform I launched in March 2013, with no (and I mean zero!) experience of the print magazine industry. I knew I was bold to launch a magazine with a global vision into a market where sales were in steady decline. I was *definitely* naïve. But in a sense, my lack of knowledge was a total blessing. I could write my own rules without being held back by the 'shoulds' of how industry veterans had always done things before me. Today, the platform – and the side projects that have sprung from it – is bigger than anything even I could have imagined.

The reason my naivety didn't matter was because I was completely and unashamedly on purpose. Every cell in my body was energised by this idea that I was onto something big. Something bigger than me, that was certain.

I built *Collective Hub* because I want to ignite human potential and create a community where entrepreneurs and creatives can inspire each other. My purpose, my personal why, is to be an entrepreneur for entrepreneurs, living my life out loud, showing that anything is possible.

Just less than a year before launch, in April 2012, the idea for *Collective Hub* landed squarely in my heart. At the time, I was still doing my 'normal' job, running a branding and marketing company, and I continued to do so as my ideas for *Collective Hub* evolved (because, real life!). It took almost 12 months for me to gather the people, resources, support and expertise I needed to get the magazine off the ground, starting with three loyal staff members who I'd worked with for years and were willing to go on this ride with me.

For an ambitious fast-thinker, 12 months felt like an extraordinarily long amount of time to birth a new business. But, for a magazine launch? A *global* magazine launch? Starting from a place of no experience to creating, designing, writing and publishing our debut issue, at a handsome six-figure cost? Some major players in the publishing industry spend that long finalising a magazine's title, let alone the entire product and strategy! I was completely green in magazine publishing, but I was also 100 per cent sure of myself as I launched a movement that, I knew in my heart, was going to change the game. And we have done exactly that, in just four years.

I knew that all the roads in my life, the ups and downs, the shifts and stages of my career had led to this point. While it may have taken me a while to find my Why, my life has transformed 180 degrees since I did.

Today, it's the single, most common question I am asked by our community:

How do I find my Why?

How can I discover my purpose?

What can I do to really connect with my goals?

How do I know that this is what I'm really meant to be doing?

I hear these questions every day. Every. Day. They land in my inbox and pop up in my social media feed. At speaking events, people always stop me afterwards to ask what the secret is to my positivity and energy.

You are what inspired me to write this book. Our *Collective Hub* community, who I try to constantly tune into so we can stay on top of what you want to explore, where you need guidance, what your pain points are and how we can help you grow.

I've written a lot of books and I thoroughly enjoy the process. However, this was a tough one because it's deeply personal on an individual level, and also incredibly hard to quantify.

As you know, my Why is about being an entrepreneur, living my life out loud, showing that anything's possible. And I believe that will not change until the day I die.

I plan to spend the rest of my life exploring, seeking and reassessing if I'm still on purpose, and continuing to step into the biggest, boldest version of my Why.

I'm grateful because I have the most amazing benchmarks confirming my Why. I know that feeling – the grounding but euphoric excitement of being aligned with your purpose. The sparkle in your mind, the joy in your heart and the hope in your soul that comes when everything in your life – past and present – perfectly aligns and you think, "It all makes sense to me now."

I have experienced those moments that make you smile, when you receive an email or text or phone call showing that you're one tiny step closer to bringing your idea to life. Those times your heart starts to race or you just have to laugh out loud at the synchronicity of it all, as suddenly everything starts to fall into place or randomly lines up…

This is how it feels to live your Why – at least, it is for me! And this is what propels me forwards, even when the going gets tough.

Living your life on purpose doesn't mean you have to change the world. Your Why can be anything, big or small. That's because it all boils down to whatever it is that makes *you* stay in flow and be the best version of yourself.

You could impact five people or five billion people. The number is irrelevant. It's about finding that connection, that drive, that will to want to do whatever it is you want to do, then pushing forwards with everything you've got.

You don't need to be an entrepreneur or innovator. Anyone and everyone can find more meaning and purpose in their lives if they connect to their Why. You could be a stay-at-home parent, a teacher, a sportsperson, an artist, a writer, a creative or an employee at a corporate company. The key is that you feel like your contribution – whatever that is – to your corner of the world matters and helps to impact people's lives in a positive way.

To find your Why, use your current life as a starting point BUT don't place any limits on where you would like it to take you. Through my work, I continue to meet extraordinary people who have completely flipped their worlds and are now doing things, both in their professional and personal lives, that their younger selves would never have imagined. That's because when searching for their Why, these people didn't place any limitations on themselves. They looked far outside their comfort zones and had the courage to chase after a dream they still didn't fully understand.

So what if you've never done it before, have no contacts in that industry or no knowledge of how it works? Neither did I! The wonderful thing about humans is that we have an innate capacity to learn, adapt, evolve and connect with other people who can fill in our knowledge gaps and help us turn our vision into reality. What could be more exciting than that?

WHY YOU, WHY NOW?

As with all of my books, I never pretend to be an expert on any subject. I'm not a psychologist or an academic, and I actually hope that this is what makes my story more relatable and my experience more helpful. This book is for anyone who has sat in an office watching the clock tick towards 6pm, willing it to go faster. Anyone who suffers from the Sunday-night blues. And anyone who has uttered the words, "Why do I put myself through this?" Yep, we've all been there!

Even now, when I can truly say I'm living my purpose – with passion and dedication – I still have moments when I make a decision based on pressure, social expectation or sheer exhaustion. But, because I know my Why – intimately – I am able to quickly realise my mistake, address it and step back onto my path of purpose once again.

I make decisions every day that I'm sure some people think are crazy. "Why is she doing *that*?" Funnily enough, I'm currently writing this book from inside a retreat that some people might describe as a cult, in India! But more on that later…

When you know your Why, you suddenly become immune to naysayers and critics because you are so sure of yourself that nobody else can make you question yourself or the path that you're on. This book is just as much for those who have found and lost their Why, as it is for those who are searching for it to begin with.

My wish for you is really quite simple. I want you to flow through each day with one clear, overarching statement that aligns everything you think, say, do, experiment with, explore and action. I want you to know why the challenges are worth it, why the hell you should keep going, you should keep exploring, and you should keep growing.

Why you, why now?

We're about to find out…

What's Their Why?

To give people
the power to
share and
make the world
more open and
connected.

FACEBOOK

———

To use business
to improve lives.

TOMS

———

To reimagine
commerce in
ways that build
a more fulfilling
and lasting
world.

ETSY

To connect
the world's
professionals
to make them
more productive
and successful.

LINKEDIN

———

To build the
best product,
cause no
unnecessary
harm, use
business to
inspire and
implement
solutions
to the
environmental
crisis.

PATAGONIA

To help bring
creative
projects to life.

KICKSTARTER

———

To enrich
people's lives
with programs
and services
that inform,
educate and
entertain.

BBC

———

To be the
company that
provides the
absolute best
service online.

ZAPPOS

To ignite human potential

COLLECTIVE HUB

WHY HAVE A WHY?

"The two most important days in your life are the day you were born
and the day you find out why."

So says a popular proverb about the importance of life purpose. Studies show
that a sense of purpose makes us more resilient, improves health, increases life
satisfaction and, according to one medical study, even helps people with chronic
conditions feel less distressed. Research from North America even found that
people who said they had a sense of purpose lived longer than those who didn't –
regardless of what age they found their Why. Need any more convincing?

Having a Why gives us direction. It gives us something to long for, to yearn for.
An end point. A reason for being. When times get tough, if you don't know why
you do what you do, it's really easy to give up, to throw it all away – and to believe
it's not actually worth all the struggle, heartache and pain.

Have you ever questioned why you put yourself *through this*?

> Why you go to the same place, day after day?

> Why you endure the same frustrations?

> Why you return to the same problems?

> Or why you feel unsure a solution even exists for you to find?

When you have a reason for being, it's so much easier to keep going. It gives you
reserves of hustle that you didn't even know you had, which give you the fight,
energy and willpower you need to move mountains and take the next step in your
journey, whatever that is. Even in the darkest, hardest moments of despair (and
there have been many for me) my Why has resonated so deeply and held so much
meaning that I simply had no choice but to keep going.

79% of leaders think their Why is central to business success, according to a PwC survey.

66% of leaders think distinction and differentiation are an important part of their organisation's purpose.

83% of employees say having meaning in their day-to-day lives is important.

Having a purpose makes you smarter!

A team of researchers from Canada and the United States surveyed 3489 adults between the ages of 32 and 84.

They found that adults who reported a greater sense of purpose in life also tended to score higher on tests of memory and overall cognition.

... And wealthier

When researchers followed the same sample of people over a period of about nine years, they found those who reported a greater sense of purpose at the study's start had a greater household income and net worth initially, and were more likely to increase these.

...It can even make you live longer!

Another study, by researchers from University College London, Princeton University and Stony Brook University, studied the lifespan of nearly 10,000 people in their sixties. They found that those people with a high sense of 'eudemonic wellbeing' – which relates to feeling like what you do is worthwhile and has purpose – lived, on average, two years longer than those with the lowest eudemonic wellbeing.

Find Your Why and
Your How Will Follow

Here's the real magic of finding your Why: once you know it, the How is unlocked.

And your How is free to move and flow, morph, iterate, pivot and change, depending on external needs.

Figuring out your Why can also be a practice you apply to your idea or your business. At *Collective Hub*, for example, I am razor sharp on our Why – it's the one and only reason we pour our hearts, souls, blood, sweat and tears into producing a full 146-page issue of the magazine each month, as well as 240 stories on the *Collective Hub* website, bespoke events, weekly masterclasses, full-day immersion workshops, year-long education courses, co-working spaces and a myriad of other offerings.

The print magazine is only about 5 per cent of the business now, which has grown into multiple platforms, touch points, mediums and mechanisms. Our delivery method is irrelevant, really, because everything we do aligns to the same Why: *Collective Hub* exists to ignite human potential. Pure and simple.

Without our Why, I honestly believe that the magazine – and everything that has grown from it – would simply fail to connect with our audience, and it would probably fall apart.

And that's what this 212-page book is ALL about – helping you to find one sentence that sums up your Why, which you can write on a Post-it note, a whiteboard in your office, the back of your hand or just imprint onto your heart.

Once you know your Why, the How has a way of working itself out.

STEP 1:
GET CLEAR ON WHO YOU ARE

What do you want in life?

What makes you tick?

What makes you come alive?

What wakes you up?

What inspires you?

What do others say about you?

What are the recurring themes in your life?

What are you good at?

What are your innate strengths?

Where do you think you add greatest value?

What's your motivation?

What do you value?

What's your personal vision?

What are your non-negotiables in life?

What do you believe in?

What makes you stand out from the crowd?

STEP 2:
MAKE INTENTIONAL SPACE
TO PUT YOUR WHY INTO WORDS

When you think about your life, your purpose, your ideas and where you see yourself heading, what kinds of thoughts and feelings come up for you? Now, these are some pretty heavy-duty questions – and you may have to take yourself out of your day-to-day grind to start answering them.

I've been known to do this myself. Let's face it; life is busy (understatement!). In the era of social media in particular, there really is no such thing as 'alone time' (home alone with my 5000 friends...) and natural moments of quiet contemplation to soul-delve have never been further out of reach. That's why it's vital to purposefully orchestrate sections of solitude and thinking time, whether it's going to sit in a park on your lunchbreak (with your phone on airplane mode), spending time in the ocean (my thinking place), or leaving the city behind for an entire weekend or longer.

In fact, when writing this book I did this in a big way!

Journal your WHY as frequently as you can manage. Daily? Weekly? Monthly? Write down your WHY statement simply and concisely and keep it somewhere you can see it daily.

The act of writing your WHY helps you define it, commit to it and start to truly step into living your life's purpose.

Define it. Commit to it. Live it!

When I was recently in India (purposefully removed geographically to another continent to ensure I had the time and space to just be...) I wrote. A lot. The ramblings, thoughts, ideas and insights that poured out of me over those days (and the weeks that followed) formed the basis of this book. They also enabled me to reconfirm my Why, which in turn enabled me to come home and enlighten and enliven my team again.

Giving myself intentional space really allowed me to journey deeper into my own personal Why and my life's purpose, which I couldn't have done in the bustle of day-to-day life. It also gave me a delightful excuse to watch, read, listen and consume everything about purpose from the greats – the people and leaders I admire. This book is a mash-up of my own personal journey, experiences, reflections and learnings from staying open and observing others. I cover a lot of ground – supported by some of my inspirational friends. In essence, I hope it is a collection of inspired ideas that help you on your journey.

As David Viscott said, "The purpose of life is to find your gift. The meaning of life is to give your gift away."

HERE ARE A FEW QUESTIONS TO HELP YOU GET STARTED

WHY ARE YOU READING THIS NOW?

WHAT ARE YOUR PASSIONS?

WHEN DO YOU FEEL MOST HAPPY?

IF MONEY DIDN'T MATTER, WHAT WOULD YOU DO FOR THE REST OF YOUR LIFE?

WHAT ARE YOU DOING TODAY THAT WILL HELP YOU BE BETTER TOMORROW?

WHAT'S ON YOUR BUCKET LIST?

WHEN YOU GET YOUR WHY RIGHT

I was recently invited to an event at one of the most prestigious fine jewellers in Australia. In fact, I wasn't just invited to attend, I was invited to host the event and they draped me in a pair of earrings worth a cool AU$50,000 and a ring worth AU$20,000.

Now, anyone who knows me will understand that I couldn't care less about the dollar figure – but who doesn't love to be showered in pretty, sparkly, glamorous things?

It was a busy, jam-packed night full of love and tears – I'll get to that later – but even amidst the chaos of that night I knew it was important to stop and acknowledge the moment.

Australia's oldest, most prestigious jewellery company was adorning me in their jewels and trusting me – yes, lil' old me – to talk on behalf of their brand. It's not about the money. It's never about the money. It's about belief. And trust. And moments. And gratitude.

During the tough times in your business, and there will be plenty of them, it's crucial that you are connected to your Why. And it's just as important – and humbling – to wear your Why on your sleeve when the going is good.

At this jewellery event I cried with gratitude at least four times, as our *Collective Hub* community came up and told me about their stories of courage and bravery, change and growth. Of how *Collective Hub*, or I, had given them the wings to fly.

This happens at almost every event I attend nowadays – people from our community share with me and I get emotional as a result! It lifts me up and inspires me in ways that I can't even explain. And it truly humbles me to know that so many people in Australia and around the world are connecting with our Why: to ignite human potential.

It also restores my faith in what we're doing and where we're headed with

Collective Hub. I mean, with feedback, impact and connections like this, who am I *not* to keep going?

When life gets tough (and oh, it does!), it's these stories, moments and connections that remind me unequivocally of my Why, and the Why that drives *Collective Hub.* So, I soak up that energy and step into it, and step up – bigger, bolder and stronger than ever.

This is why I ask myself every single day: why am I doing this?

I know my answer. And now it's time for me to throw the question out to you.

When you wake up tomorrow – as you step out of bed, boot up your laptop, check your emails and prepare to tackle your to-do list – take a breath, take a moment, pause and think about why you're dedicating your day to these actions.

The average person will spend 90,000 hours at work over their lifetime. Don't you deserve to know why?

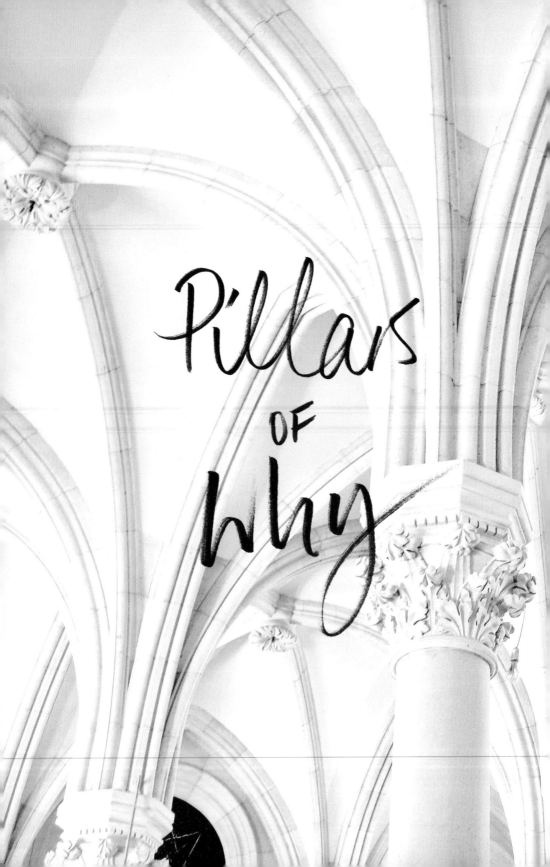

Pillars
of
why

Your Why has the power to unearth extraordinary and unexplainable things. Call it faith, call it purpose, call it Why. It doesn't matter what you call it.

Your Why is what keeps you going when you feel like you're at your absolute limits and in the depths of despair.

Your Why is the one thing that propels you forwards in times of success and happiness, and in times of failure and rejection.

The world around you may change – but your Why won't.

Your Why is more important than your How. Once you know your Why, you can move and flow, morph, iterate, pivot or change as your external circumstances do.

You are never too old – or too young – to find and live out your Why.

The single most important part of finding your Why is learning not to interrupt its growth in your life. You simply have to let it flow.

There is no shortcut to finding your Why. Once you've found it, don't overthink it. Just get started.

You might want to create a life worth living, but the secret element to achieving that is YOU.

Your Why can be big or small – that doesn't matter – the key is finding out what makes you live a life of flow so you're the best version of yourself.

Once you know your Why, it's paramount that you help others along on their journeys. Purpose works when it is BIGGER than you. Be authentic, open and honest about your search. Live your life out loud!

a
big,
wonderful,
happy, fulfilling
life is out there

and 100% available
to anyone who has
the vision,
strength and
courage
to make it so.

part 1.

THE POWER OF

PURPOSE

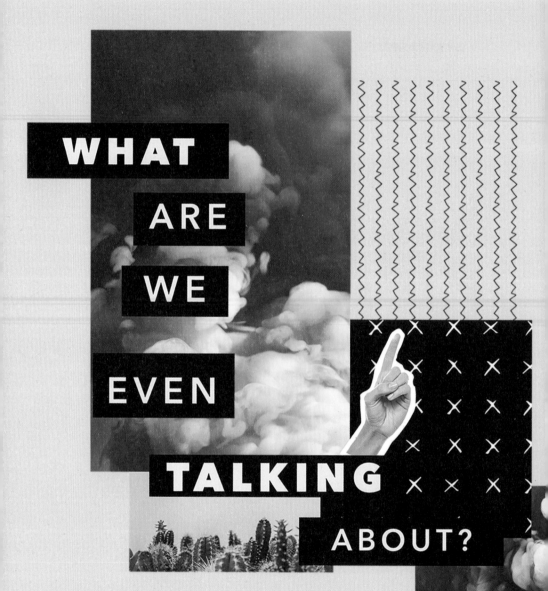

WHAT THE HELL IS PURPOSE ANYWAY?

Your Why: it's something that connects and resonates so deeply at your core, something that you feel so strongly in every single cell of your body, that when you finally find it you can't imagine what you ever did before.

It is *so much* bigger than you. When it lands, it just feels effortless, like it's the most natural thing in the world for you to do. It shouldn't be something forced and it shouldn't be overthought.

It should just land and flow, easily and naturally.

It might come to you in the middle of the night, as you stand in the shower or while you wait for an elevator. It might be triggered by something you see, a conversation you have or a combination of events, memories and meetings that compound into an idea that feels like the missing jigsaw piece in your life.

It might feel like it comes out of nowhere but, when you explore it, examine it, dig out its roots and dissect it, you will probably find that it is not entirely new.

It might not be the most obvious thing when it lands – it might not even be the thing you thought you were working towards. But in hindsight, it will all make perfect sense. Once you sink into your Why, you'll be absolutely amazed at how your life shifts, how incredible new doors open up, how opportunities you hadn't dared to even dream of suddenly fall within reach.

When I found my Why, everything changed. It seemingly happened out of nowhere, but the more I reflected on it, it made absolute, complete sense to me. It was exactly what I had been (unconsciously) building towards my entire life. And I do mean: my *entire* life!

When I put pen to paper in 2014 for *Daring & Disruptive*, my first book in this series, I wrote a whole chapter called 'Know Your Why'. In it, I cover how my Why came from a long series of events over many years – most of them associated with immense emotional pain points or frustrations – coupled with a true sense of

Words will never do it justice to express how deep and ready my call was. I literally said to the universe:

> "If the best use of me is cleaning toilets in India for the rest of my life, then I will do it."

It was the greatest moment of letting go and surrendering I have ever experienced in my entire life. I figuratively surrendered every single cell in my body to whatever the universe had in store.

I just knew I was ready for the next step. And then one day, the idea dropped into my lap:

> I needed to build a community of like-minded people who were clever, informed, creative and world-changing.

It would start with a magazine... and so we did it!

EXCERPT FROM
DARING & DISRUPTIVE.

surrender, stillness and detachment from outcome on my part. In short, these two paragraphs from that chapter encapsulate how it was for me.

The career you chose, the skills you learnt, the mistakes you made, the failures you faced and the people you've met along the way haven't been wasted – in fact, it's quite the opposite.

Every little thing you have worked at, started, experienced, loved, learnt from and been challenged by, all of these experiences are culminating together in one perfect bundle that will form your Why from this point onwards.

I don't dislike the person I was before I discovered my Why. It's crucial that you're grateful for all your life stages, all the people you've been and the transformations you've experienced. So what if you spent 10 years in a job that didn't ignite you? Who cares if you committed to the wrong career or chose a university degree that didn't turn out to be your vocation? Stop feeling sorry for yourself or wishing you'd acted differently.

ALL ROADS HAVE LED YOU
TO THIS DESTINATION
—EVEN IF YOU DON'T KNOW
EXACTLY WHERE YOU ARE YET!

WHO WERE YOU 10 YEARS AGO?

WHO WERE YOU 5 YEARS AGO?

WHO WERE YOU 12 MONTHS AGO?

WHO DO YOU WANT TO BE TOMORROW?

Looking Back ⇌
Propels You Forwards

When I look back at my life, absolutely nothing makes sense in a linear order. I never set out to start a magazine and I didn't plot out my career to help me gravitate to this point. But in a nonsensical way, after it all came together, everything I have ever done makes perfect sense and has undoubtedly put me on the path towards living my Why today.

As singular units in time, each of my experiences don't appear to be linked or even the slightest bit integral to my life now, as the founder of a global media and education movement.

I was a horse-riding instructor in the country. I was a corporate events manager. I managed sponsorships for big brands, such as The Wiggles and Cirque Du Soleil. I launched and ran my own small business – a content creation, branding and marketing company.

I even worked in politics for a brief stint. When I was 23, I held 13 voluntary positions simultaneously for the Liberal Party. This had less to do with my political beliefs and more to do with gaining an incredible grounding in leadership, passion and the power of persuasion. I learnt *a lot* at this time in my life, including the fact that it's easier to rise up through the ranks with voluntary positions than it is to ascend through paid roles. I chose not to pursue an actual political career, but many people I sat alongside in those days went on to secure prominent positions – including Gladys Berejiklian, the Premier of New South Wales at the time of writing.

These experiences all appear to be completely separate and unique, in no way, shape or form linked to my role now. However, when I look back I can start to see the links in the chain…

Growing up in the country probably made me quite grounded and prepared me for stepping into the world I move in now, which can be over-the-top and unbelievable at times. Working in events taught me how to multitask and juggle a million things at once, which is crucial to what I'm doing now. While *Collective Hub* started as a magazine, our events are a major business extension and add so much value to our community.

Working in sponsorship for The Wiggles and other arts and entertainment properties was the best possible on-the-job training of my life. It gave me absolutely essential grounding to broker the big deals I'm doing now with *Collective Hub*!

These are just a handful of my experiences and they have all, in their own surprising way, prepared me for what was to come.

LOVE EVERY LIFE STAGE!

The truth is that we are all in transition – whether we can see it or not at the time. Our lives are made up of pivots, twists, turns and adjustments, which hopefully lead to contentment, satisfaction and that warm glow of pride – if we follow our own paths and don't allow distractions, societal pressures and self-doubt to sway us off track.

It's not only the sum of our professional experiences that shape us, either. I've been (very!) open in my past books about the personal milestones that have moulded me as an entrepreneur. Going through a divorce, drinking too much, giving up drinking 13 years ago, becoming estranged from members of my family, reuniting with them again. Love, loss and burnout have all made me strong enough, tenacious enough and resilient enough to deal with what came next.

If you haven't quite landed on your Why yet, that's fine – don't dwell on it and don't be hard on yourself. The most important thing to focus on now is that you're finally ready to start really digging deep to connect to your purpose.

Nothing that you have done in the past is wrong. It was where you needed to be at that point in time, in that headspace, to fill your cup with the experiences that have led you forwards to this moment.

The question is: where will you go from here?

Why Didn't I Do This Before?

The journey I'm on now was a lifetime in the making, [but] it was only ready to launch when I became truly and 100% connected with my Why.

When you find your Why, it can seem so obvious, such a natural fit, that you might wonder, "Why didn't I do this before?"

I can tell you why. You weren't ready.

There's no freaking way I would have been strong enough to do this any earlier in my life. The specific moment that we launched the magazine, in March 2013, was always meant to be the moment of lift-off.

It doesn't matter that I attended the Frankfurt Book Fair in 2007 and afterwards in Marrakesh, I sat and scribbled down a sketchy business plan for a series of magazines that I could develop. (I dive deeper into my crazy Moroccan experience in my book *Daring & Disruptive.*)

It doesn't matter that I bought a book a short while later, called *How to Start a Magazine.*

It doesn't matter that I actually registered the business name 'Messenger Magazines' a full two years before I even got the idea for *Collective Hub*!

None of these things mean that I should have started my journey into magazine publishing earlier.

Instead, all of these moments prove that, while the journey I'm on now was a lifetime in the making, it was only ready to launch when I became truly and 100 per cent connected with my Why.

One of the most significant pieces of the puzzle that clicked when my Why landed was this fact: all the experiences I had garnered over the years had purpose. All the heartache and the hard times happened for a reason. These challenges and missteps and moments that, at the time, sank me to my knees and made me struggle to even get out of bed in the morning, were the exact same experiences that made me strong enough to step into this big, bold, exciting, exhilarating, crushing space I find myself in today.

Also, they were a catalyst – I knew from my own prior struggles with inadequacies, fear, lack of support and overwhelming self-doubt that there was a market need for *Collective Hub*. Better still, I knew I was strong enough to step in and help others. This was my calling – I could literally feel it in my gut.

In many ways, you could say that *Collective Hub* is a 16-year overnight success. I had a publishing and marketing business for 11 years, while I daydreamed about stepping into something bigger, bolder and more impactful. What was I doing for all of that time, if not preparing to launch this magazine and gearing up for this moment?

WHAT MOMENTS HAVE LED YOU HERE?

That job or promotion
you didn't get...

Outcomes and experiences
you'd rather forget...

Travel and trips that took
you in a different direction...

People you met who changed
the course of your life...

Challenges and hiccups
in your career...

Plans gone awry at home
or at work...

What have you learnt from each part of your journey?

What skills, experiences, expertise, drive and resilience have these moments gifted you?

How have those experiences changed you, educated you and propelled you forwards?

Do you need a Why?

Your Why End Game?

To settle on one overarching
statement for your life that
you will live by, encapsulating
why you are on this planet
and why you will be who
you are and act how you do.

WORD FROM THE WHYS: SEBASTIAN TERRY

I love people who know what they want – and go out and get it. I first heard about Sebastian Terry, creator of the '100 Things' project, on social media. The blogger and author is on a mission to complete 100 items on his bucket list, while raising AU$100,000 for Camp Quality – an organisation that creates happiness for children and families affected by cancer. His adventures have led to a best-selling book, a documentary series and a lot of do-goodery (one of the items on his list was to push a wheelchair user around a half marathon). Seb and I have become great friends in our shared passion for purpose.

Here's what Seb has to say about the subject...

"As much as we'd all like to close our eyes, think hard and suddenly realise our true reason for being here, purpose, I've found, is something that can only be found through experience, consideration and honesty.

"As we navigate life, we are buoyed by our passions and influenced by environment, experiences and people, but it's purpose that creates the elusive third dimension to life; it gives us reason. It's our overarching Why and allows us to connect with the world outside of just ourselves.

"Living *with* purpose stems from being able to live on purpose, and this of course requires an understanding of our values, our beliefs and what we stand for.

"Do you know who you really are?

"Purpose doesn't have to be grand and it doesn't have to be world-changing, it just has to reflect *you*. It's not defined by *what* we do or *how* we do it, but rather *why* we do it. It transcends societal labels, money and all other tangible items, and falls across all aspects of our life. In this sense, our profession, relationships, interests and goals are not individual platforms but a collective that should all be contributing in some way towards our overarching purpose.

"When we live in this way – on purpose – time and energy seem boundless, as clarity, resourcefulness and drive filter into all that we do.

"Purpose, if I'm honest, is something I'm still working on today. I know, for example, that I'm passionate about helping others and that this excites me more than anything else. I didn't know this when I began my own 100 Things journey in 2009.

"Does that mean that *helping others* is my purpose? Maybe. What I know is more important than being able to define it, though, is being able to go to sleep at night and feel a warm buzz, because I know what I did today, and what I'll do tomorrow, will contribute to me growing and learning about what it is I'm here to do. The on-flow of this is that I'm able to be of service to the greater good – not just my own.

"Purpose is not a science and there is no quick equation to calculate your own. It's all about the journey and every step is a valuable one."

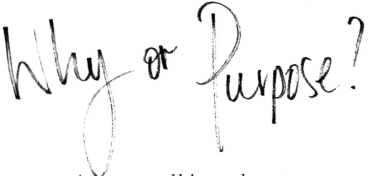

Why or Purpose?

Are we talking about
the same thing here?

Are Why and Purpose
one and the same?

Same, same or different?

Oh, the semantics!

Call it what you like,
but for me they are one
and the same – the key is not
to waste too much energy
talking about it or defining it,
just go out and find it.

YOU LOVE IT

Passion

Mission

YOU ARE
GREAT AT IT

THE WORLD
NEEDS IT

Profession

Vocation

YOU ARE
PAID FOR IT

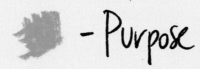 — Purpose

THIS IS YOUR

KICK UP THE ARSE:

THINK ABOUT

WHY YOU DO

WHAT YOU DO.

A Life Worth Living

What gets you out of bed each morning? When you have a purpose-led life, you know the answer to this question immediately, undoubtedly, because your answer is rooted in your Why.

Take this as your kick up the arse, your call to arms, your wake-up warning, your reminder that there are no dress rehearsals and that the time to take action and do something is NOW!

Get excited about living a life that counts, a life of service and gratitude and experience – a life that you will look back on with pride in your old age and think, "Yep, I did that."

WORD FROM THE WHYS: PETER BAINES

Choice. What it's all about.

When I think of the people I know who are unequivocally living their Why, I think of Peter Baines. He is truly making an impact in this world, every single day. I flew one of my writers to Thailand many years ago to support publishing Pete's first book, and last year I spent time in one of the orphanages he supports.

As a police forensic specialist, Peter was working in Thailand with the victim identification team following the tragic 2004 Boxing Day tsunami. He was deeply touched by the number of children left homeless and alone in the aftermath, and felt compelled to establish an organisation that could make a real difference to their lives.

In late 2005, Peter stepped into his Why and co-founded Hands Across the Water. Today, the charity is in its 12th year and has grown to support and create long-term opportunities for 300 at-risk children across Thailand. What's the driving force that keeps Peter connected to doing what he does? *Choice.*

> "*Choice* is one of our key values. I find that word so central to everything we do. How does the number of homes we build, the dollars we raise or the bike rides that we organise speak to *choice* for the children we support?

> "If our kids spend 5, 7 or 10 years with us and upon leaving one of our homes, find that their choices are limited, have we really been successful? If the boys find themselves working in a rubber plantation for AU$6 a day, and the girls in a bar or worse, have we really provided them with *choice*?

"If that is the outcome, I would suggest we've failed them.

"The measure of our impact, the difference we have made, is really only realised when the kids leave our homes – when, because of the education they have received, they have true *choice* about their life.

"If they leave educated, equipped and *choice* abounds them, and they *choose* rubber plantation or bar work, then we have done the best we can.

"We have 46 kids now at various universities across Thailand, studying courses from science and agriculture, to business and tourism, to English literature to Chinese business. This is surely a measure of impact and leading these kids down a path of *choice*. If this is the outcome, I would suggest we're succeeding."

What choices do you have in your life ... and where are your choices leading you?

IT'S ALL A MATTER OF CHOICE

Consider: what's the greatest gift you have to offer and how can you tap into that gift to make your mark?

Being a 'Doer' or a 'Gunna'

"I'll launch the business if..."

"I would do it, if only..."

"I'm just waiting for the perfect moment..."

Everyone has ideas. But what separates those of us who live in the blissful, purpose-led space of living our Why from everybody else is simple: less talk and more action.

You can't blame anyone but yourself if, when your aha moment happens, you scribble a life-changing idea on a page in your notebook, stick it in your desk drawer and let it gather dust under your bitten pens, paper clips and chocolate wrappers.

I have written in the past about my frustration with 'gunnas' – you know, the people who say they're 'gunna' do something, but never quite get around to it. They haven't seen a sign, the timing isn't right, their boss just needs them for one more project, and how could they possibly quit on them?

Fast-forward two years: someone else has launched their 'unique' idea and revolutionised an industry, while the 'gunna' is still staring at the faded wall of their cubicle.

This might sound harsh. And I'm the first to admit that it takes a huge amount of courage to chase your Why. Especially when it means stepping away from a comfortable existence – a stable job (if there is such a thing these days), a good salary, a company car. I understand why it can feel safer to stay on the ledge, instead of leaping.

But people leap every day. I know because I meet them!

- The single dad who left his job to join a tech start-up

- The 16-year-old health blogger who convinced her school to sponsor her

- The 83-year-old grandmother who developed her own prototype

- The corporate intrapreneur who pitched her innovation idea to her boss

These are the 'doers', who don't just have a brainwave and brush it aside. Instead, they instigate it, innovate it, action it and implement it. They could build roadblocks, make excuses and join the 'gunnas' on their road to nowhere, but instead, they take their first step on the adventure of a lifetime.

The truth is, there will always be a good excuse not to fulfil your purpose. It will never be the perfect time, the stars will never perfectly align and there probably won't be a sign. If you're waiting, you'll be waiting forever. Every forward-thinker feels fear, trepidation and apprehension. It's a natural side effect of innovation. But later, you'll find regret is a far harder emotion to digest.

So, WHO ARE YOU GOING TO BE: A DOER OR A GUNNA?

You can make a small impact across many areas, or you can find your true course – your **Why**...

...and turn your impact into something **truly magnificent**.

STYLE MAKERS

IRIS APFEL

This fashion icon has lived a life of style and substance. After building a career as an interior stylist, Iris was catapulted into mainstream stardom at the age of 84 as an international style phenomenon. She ditches rules in favour of originality, and her unwavering devotion to all things style is testament that your life passion can really become a reality – even at age 95. "All of these wonderful projects fell into my lap," she says. "Designing a cosmetic line, doing eyewear and all this kind of stuff. I've never retired. I think retirement is a fate worse than death."

GRACE CODDINGTON

With her magnificent artistic vision and long legacy of working behind-the-scenes at *Vogue* – side by side with none other than Anna Wintour – Grace has spent years covering each page of the iconic magazine with her creative fingerprints, influencing generations of fashionistas along the way.

SARAH JESSICA PARKER

SJP and her renowned character Carrie Bradshaw on *Sex and the City* have been impressively influential on the world of fashion. Sarah Jessica's image, both on and off screen, continues to push boundaries.

RULE BREAKERS

SIR RICHARD BRANSON

A visionary! Pure and simple. This man has taken entrepreneurship to astronomical heights – quite literally in regards to *Virgin Galactic* – via his suite of Virgin companies across a multitude of industries, from music to gyms and from planes to space.

OSHO

Shedding mystic light on topics that are traditionally considered taboo, the Indian guru and spiritual leader of the Rajneesh movement, Osho, inspired thousands (if not millions) of people to think differently.

NELSON MANDELA

Revolutionary, philanthropist and advocate for human rights, this man helped bring an end to apartheid in South Africa after serving jail time for standing by his values. He showed his nation and the world the transforming power of forgiveness as South Africa's first post-apartheid President.

THOUGHT LEADERS

MAHATMA GANDHI

The voice and symbol of the non-violent civil action movement, who changed the face of resistance forever.

BILL & MELINDA GATES

The world's ultimate power couple, raising the bar for billionaires everywhere when it comes to giving back. After co-founding Microsoft, Bill joined forces with his wife to form the Bill & Melinda Gates Foundation, which is generously and altruistically tackling tough global issues, such as extreme poverty, health in the developing world and failing education systems.

MICHELLE OBAMA

As former First Lady of the United States, Michelle made leaps and bounds in implementing healthy-living strategies to combat childhood obesity and empowering girls' education – all with grace, intelligence and eloquence.

Doers to Move You...

GAME CHANGERS

ELON MUSK

The visionary CEO
of Tesla and SpaceX is
reshaping our perception
of transportation – on
Earth and in space.

STEVE JOBS

The man at the epicentre of the digital revolution,
the co-founder of Apple revolutionised the very
idea of technology's role and capabilities
in everyday life.

OPRAH WINFREY

A global, inspirational
personal brand, Oprah
is an influential talk
show host and media
icon. She is also a keen
philanthropist, with the
power and influence to
impact millions.

Lessons I Learnt from
My Own Funeral

I drove myself to my funeral. That's not something that many people can say! But

As I lay down by that gravestone to reflect on what my funeral would look like, it was a profoundly confronting experience – one that would change my life forever.

in 2004, when I enrolled in a life-changing self-development program at one of my lowest points, that's exactly what I did. Let me explain…

This course uses various techniques and borrows from many different belief systems and philosophies – from Eastern mysticism and deep meditation to group therapy, visualisation and more – with the goal of condensing a lifetime of analysis into just eight days. No mean feat, right?

On this particular morning, the last day of our program, we were told nothing about where we were going, what we were doing or what was happening next – the exact formula that had been rolled out over the previous seven days. (It was a wonderful life lesson in trust, surrender and letting go, a concept I'll cover in more depth in part two.)

The next thing I knew, a series of black, sombre cars pulled up. If I didn't know better, I would have thought we were off to a funeral, as they gave off a distinctly morbid and solemn vibe.

"How strange", I thought as I silently hopped into the car... Only it wasn't strange. It was spot on. A funeral was *exactly* where we were going. The really interesting part was, it was our own funeral we were going to *and* we were driving ourselves there.

If that doesn't blow your hair back, I don't know what will!

So there we were, not allowed to talk, completely in silence, getting into funeral procession cars with a bunch of strangers we'd met only days before. In hindsight, the drama of it is what made it so incredibly impactful.

When we arrived at the cemetery – yes, a real cemetery, no props or pretending – we climbed out of our black cars and were told to go silently and find a gravestone that would represent us. I walked around the cemetery with an open mind, looking for a gravestone so I could lie down next to it and pretend I was... dead.

I remember feeling strangely calm as I lay down and made myself comfortable on my, ahem, gravesite. In reality, I should not have felt calm. My life up until that moment (let's call it 'pre-cemetery experience') was pretty much the greatest train smash you could imagine. I was drinking myself into a stupor most days, I was in a marriage with a guy I had nothing in common with[*] and I hadn't spoken to any of my family for three years. I had no semblance of who I was and I felt truly, in every possible definition of the word, lost.

[*]He was a sweetheart (I just had work to do).

As I lay down by that gravestone to reflect on what my funeral would look like, it was a profoundly confronting experience – one that would change my life forever.

For those of you who know me as the 'Lisa Messenger' of today, what I am about to tell you is a far cry from where I am now. Hopefully, it serves to truly show you that anything is possible and anyone can change and evolve their situation.

As I lay there picturing my own funeral, I could imagine possibly 10 people (at best) hovering above me, shaking their heads, saying, "It was only a matter of time." I was on such a journey of self-sabotage and depression that in my mind, at that time, I assumed my funeral followed my suicide. There was no legacy to be left – only disappointment, shame and a sense of waste.

In that moment – and it gives me shivers writing it now – I decided absolutely, unequivocally, *to turn my life around*.

Now, I'm not saying you need to do something as dramatic as this in order to shake things up and start asking the deeper questions to get to your authentic truth! But, I am a huge advocate of becoming comfortable with being uncomfortable, of putting ourselves in purposefully counterintuitive situations on the path towards living our best and brightest life.

- When all is said and done and you've breathed your last breath, what will your impact be?

- What legacy will you have created?

- What will people say about you?

- What contribution will you have made in this world?

These are big questions. They can be confronting to ask yourself, and even more confronting to answer. While the answers can be uncomfortably revealing, they can also be incredibly empowering. That's because the best thing about imagining your funeral now is that you're still full of life and have the power to change it. Don't waste a single breath!

PURPOSE

OVERNIGHT SUCCESS
IS A MYTH.

YOU WANT TO SUCCEED?

SHOW UP
EVERY DAY, EVERY WEEK,
EVERY MONTH, EVERY YEAR,

WHEN NO ONE
ELSE WANTS TO.

AND WATCH WHAT HAPPENS.

YOU'LL BE THE VICTOR,

YOU'LL BE THE WINNER,

YOU'LL TASTE SUCCESS.

Who Are You Without a Why?

Suddenly
it all falls into place

There have been several times in my life when I didn't feel like I had a purpose, none more prevalent than when I was in my twenties. I was a born optimist and I've always had a certain excitement for life, but in my twenties it was misguided because I had no direction to channel my energy. I had no semblance of who I was. I was largely living life according to other people's expectations, conforming to societal norms of who I should be, and bending to other people's belief systems and values.

This can be quite a complex, multifaceted psychological topic. And it's one I have spent years and years exploring, through many awakenings, personal development programs and spiritual experiences. In essence, most of us go along gathering belief systems and certain conditioning, depending on our upbringing and surroundings. These continue to pile up and it takes a LOT of work to actually be courageous enough to stop and ask: Why am I doing/thinking/feeling/believing this? Is this really reflective of me? Are these my belief systems or have I taken them on over the years from others?

Without a Why, you can live your entire life like this, meandering through life, ungrounded, untethered, not quite knowing what your purpose is, or whether anything you do is *ever* going to make an impact.

It takes *a lot* of work to get real and authentic and strip back all the layers. To really take a good hard internal look and ask: Who am I? Like really, who am I?

I started this exploration in my twenties. For me, this was a decade or so of feeling lost and like I didn't really fit in. I know this to be the case for many others, because since I've been brave and open enough to share my experience, thousands of people have poured their hearts out to me with similar stories.

We're all a little lost in life, I think. We're all making it up as we go along. Becoming chameleons, depending on our situation and surroundings. And eventually, we find our Why. We get brave and we say, 'That's not who I am.' And suddenly, it all falls into place.

Uncomfortable. Tough. Intrusive. Challenging. You'll only get powerful answers if you're willing to ask yourself probing questions. *Who am I? Why?*

Rituals

TO RECONNECT
WITH YOUR

Why

(AND YOURSELF!)

OSHO MEDITATION

I have around
50 different
meditations that
I rotate every
day, depending
on my mood.

A NOURISHING

green smoothie
or juice every
single morning.
This is a
non-negotiable.

CHECK-IN

with grounding
relationships.
I feel completely
re-energised
by one-on-one
time with my
favourite people.

DOWNTIME

walking with my
dog, Benny; chilling
out at home.

BARRE BODY

as often as possible.
It's an amazing
fusion of Pilates,
vinyasa yoga
and ballet barre
conditioning – and
keeps me flexible
and energetic.

SLEEP

8–10 hours every
night. I don't
have kids, so I'm
fortunate to be
able to do this,
and it's why I have
buckets of energy.

BREATHE

purposefully, slowly,
intentionally.

MY 'THANK YOU' RITUAL

I say it so often,
dozens of times a
day, that it's become
an expression of
gratitude that flows
out unconsciously.
When I catch a
green light, when a
car park opens up in
front of a building
when I'm running
late for a meeting,
when a staff
member puts out a
fire for me before it
truly gets going…

The Power of Your Vision

Having a Why is about more than simply knowing what you want in life.
It's about connecting to a vision, a higher purpose, a greater reason for being
than simply meandering through each day.

If you've read any of my previous books you'll know I'm a BIG fan of visioning
techniques, whether it's vision boards, visualisation exercises or just changing my
computer screensaver to an image that inspires me. And I'm not the only one!

Years before she became an iconic entrepreneur, Sara Blakely used to imagine
sitting on Oprah Winfrey's couch on her television show, telling her story.
And Sara got there! It's a common technique for athletes, who imagine themselves
winning a race long before they've physically stepped up to the starting line.

For me, the power of vision is vital. My vision board is the place where I craft
the life of my dreams – in glorious technicolour. It's a canvas where I can collage
all the events, sights, feelings and achievements that I hope to include in my life.
And on tough days, or when I feel like I'm losing my way, it acts as a prompt
and a reminder of the Why I'm working for.

For you, the best way to vision might be cutting and sticking magazine clippings
onto a huge piece of paper (my favourite), using Pinterest to collate images that
speak to you, or just sitting in silence – imagining yourself accepting an award,
receiving your first order or sitting on the couch of the most-watched talk show
host on the planet.

If you can see it, you're one step closer to achieving it!

Let's get crafty

1. GRAB YOUR OLD COPIES OF *COLLECTIVE HUB* MAGAZINE.

2. SEARCH THROUGH OUR PAGES, WAITING FOR PICTURES, HEADLINES OR QUOTES THAT EVOKE POSITIVE EMOTION.

3. CUT, STICK AND COLLAGE.

4. PLACE IT SOMEWHERE IN YOUR HOUSE WHERE YOU'LL SEE IT ON A DAILY BASIS.

BE INSPIRED!

I just THREW myself out there back in the day. I was RELENTLESS and PERSISTENT and wore my heart on my sleeve. If you REALLY work hard and put YOURSELF out there, MAGIC happens.

Positive mind.
Positive vibes.
Positive life.

—Unknown

THE ART OF REINVENTION

where in the WORLD

game changers | thought leaders | rule breakers | style makers

ISSUE 47

COLLECTIVE HUB

HOW TO DOWNSIZE, **DECLUTTER** & REFOCUS

mindfulness
THE NEXT BILLION
DOLLAR INDUSTRY

KAFTAN QUEEN

THE
Red Box
EXERCISE

I am an avid drawer. In our office we have floor-to-ceiling glass walls – over an entire 600 sq. m floor – quite purposefully, because it means that every single wall is a blank canvas for me and my team to scribble all over. I have mind maps and ideas scrawled everywhere. Pretty much whenever I have a meeting, I like to be up and animated, drawing a visual depiction of what I'm talking about.

Now if you were in my office, you would see every criss-cross variable of what the *Collective Hub* vision looks like – circular mind maps with our various extensions, horizontal end-to-end trips from inspiration to education, as well as the recent addition of the red box. Right now, the red box is blank. I drew it just a week ago, and at the moment it's one of the most powerful pieces in my business.

You see, four years into the *Collective Hub* journey, I knew that we were missing a big piece of self-perpetuating community. Something really sticky. I could describe the feeling and what 'it' represents from a high-level perspective, but I didn't know entirely what it looked like, yet.

Within 24 hours of drawing the empty red box on my wall, the most extraordinary things started happening. I had three meetings with three different people: someone I coincidentally ran into at a big celebratory lunch; a *Collective Hub* advisory board member who I had a personal breakfast catch-up with; and one of the smartest guys I've ever met, who said he'd been trying to get a meeting with me for two years. He'd seen me speak at an event three months before and it just happened that it was THIS day – the day after I drew the infamous red box – that he came to meet with me.

Three BIG, totally unrelated meetings within 24 hours with three different people that were *all* variations on the same conversation and theme: what I thought the red box should be. This might all sound esoteric, but it's about manifestation. Sometimes in life, in my experience, when something is potentially so big, ALL you need to do is create space for it, acknowledge it, then surrender to it and let the rest start to play out.

I have had countless moments like these in my life and, in particular, in the past four years. Times when I make conscious room for something but detach from the outcome, and then experience a whole series of aha moments.

The funny thing is that the better you get at this, the more fun you can start to have with it. The red box is purposefully arrogant, much to my executive team's initial horror. How embarrassing to have that scrawled on my wall for anyone who walks into my office to see! But the thing about that is, I'm sending a loud and clear message to the Universe that this idea is big, and I'm unafraid of its magnitude.

Sometimes things are so big and so magical we're almost sorry and scared we put them out there. But that, my friends, is where the magic starts to happen. Out there on the razor's edge. Now, let's see what happens with my red box…

Sometimes things are so big
and so magical we're almost sorry
and scared we put them out there.
But that, my friends, is where
the magic starts to happen.

Understand that the right is a sacred privilege.

to choose your own path
Use it.   Dwell in possibility.

– OPRAH WINFREY

You're Never Too Much

You're never, ever, too much of anything. If there's one thing I believe firmly to be true, with every single cell of my being, it's this fact.

You are never too young or too old or too inexperienced to do anything in this life. I am living proof of this – I launched a magazine with absolutely *no* magazine experience.

Almost every week, I meet people who think that their circumstances are beyond changing, because they're too old, too uneducated, too far away geographically, too busy with family, too blocked in by the glass ceiling, too connected, too disconnected, too much of an outsider in the industry, too this, too that...

There is no right or wrong time for anything. And you're never too much. Period. Ever.

If it aligns with your purpose, then you sure as hell should pursue it.

Blockages And Limitations

Last New Year's Eve I spent time with two relatives, aged 71 and 7. I asked them both the same question: if you could have *anything* this year, what would it be? The 71-year-old struggled with the question and gave me a broad, general answer: "I want all my friends and family to be healthy and happy." But the seven-year-old? She took the task on with so much vigour and excitement that she proceeded to describe every minute detail to me. "I want to have a house in the clouds with a suction pipe down to mummy's house, so that she can send food up every day. Then I'm going to have an orange slippery slide filled with rainbows that takes me to Aunty Li Li's house, Grandpa John's house and Daddy's house. I'm going to have my own dog and my own cat…"

And on and on and on she went.

She had absolutely no limitations on herself. Zero! What a wonderfully positive and kind place to dwell in, where you believe everything is not only possible, but that it downright deserves a place in your future!

Then, with a completely serious face, she asked me, "Now, how do we make this happen?"

I had forgotten to explain the crucial part of the question – we're just dreaming, rather than making concrete plans. But I had to give her top marks for enthusiasm!

In fact, it was beyond beautiful to witness. So much so that I got an illustrator to draw up her vision so I could frame it and put it on her wall – so she will never forget the power of imagination.

CLEAR BAD JUJU

Positive mantras can help you find your Why,
keep your purpose in check, and move past
blockages and limitations:

I follow my own true path
and let others follow theirs.

I trust my purpose to lead me towards
happiness and wellbeing.

I am waiting patiently for the revelation
of my purpose.

Every moment of every day, I am becoming
more and more certain of where I need to be.

I always follow my heart's path.

Each and every day I make positive choices to take
me one step further towards where I want to be.

I surround myself with positive relationships
and let negativity wash over me.

YOU
ARE IN CHARGE OF YOUR LIFE.

YOU
ARE RESPONSIBLE
FOR YOUR OWN DESTINY.

YOU
ARE NOT TOO YOUNG OR TOO OLD
TO START OR STOP SOMETHING.

Have you stopped dreaming?

DREAM
BIGGER
AND
BIGGER
AND
BIGGER

AND
BIGGER

part 2.

HOW TO FIND YOUR

Your Why – That Elusive Little Beast...

By the end of this book, my greatest hope is that you'll start to see some big themes and pictures emerge about why you are here and what you have been put on this earth to do. You know, the little questions in life...

Sometimes people make offhand comments to me like, "Look at your life, Lisa – you're so *lucky*," or "Wow, Lisa, that must have been so much fun – what a fortunate life you lead!" I agree that I live a blessed and fortunate life. But make no mistake: it did not happen by accident. No way, no how!

Finding your Why is not going to just *happen* to you or for you. To do, see, live and experience extraordinary things, you have to be willing to put yourself out there, to take big risks, challenge yourself (daily!) and innovate and invigorate every way that you think, act and feel. Sound like hard work? It is! But, it's one hell of a ride.

I've made countless (conscious and unconscious) sacrifices in zillions of different ways – some tiny and insignificant, some big and meaningful – to reach this point in my life where I can not only identify my Why, but also turn my vision into action.

I'm not going to sugar-coat it for you, this 'finding your Why' business. It's not going to be easy. It's going to take time and work and effort and, inevitably, there will be some pain involved.

But one thing I can promise you is this: it will be worth it in the end. I guarantee it.

how do I get it?

i want it... now, how do i get it?

I'm Sold, I Want In. Now, How Do I Go About Finding My Why?

You want to find your Why. You know it's close, nearby; it's been hanging around the fringes for months, maybe years, waiting for you to gather the courage and strength and energy to tackle it with two hands.

Or perhaps it's going to be a complete surprise to you. I always knew that I wanted to connect with people in a meaningful way and create a platform for others to shine, innovate and grow. But, never in a million years did I imagine that the platform I would choose to launch with would be a global magazine. So, you never quite know what form your Why will take, do you?

How can you find it? *There are so many different ways*. Essentially – and here's the bad news – there isn't a shortcut, quick fix, pill or elixir. You need to put in the work and feel into what you love.

What makes you feel good? What feels effortless and in flow (even when it's hard)? What kind of projects and tasks make you excited to tackle them (things that strengthen you)? And what makes you retract, feel small or uninspired (things that weaken you)?

It's often said that we teach what we need to learn, so what are you missing in your own life?

What are, or have been, your pain points in life – mental, emotional, physical or otherwise?

What do people say you are good at?

Do you thrive when offering acts of service?

Do you like to connect with people?

Do people refer to you as a natural 'helper' or 'giver'?

Are you more content to work on your own, behind the scenes, offering the kind of meaningful, yet anonymous or background help that supports people to lead better lives?

Diving deeper here: what are all the experiences in your life that have led you to this point?

I want you to get gritty and really think about the hard, uninspiring, challenging, uncomfortable and even cringe-worthy or shameful experiences of your life. *Trust me* when I say that this is where the gold is.

This next point is almost counterintuitive but so very, very important. As you work through these questions, don't overthink the answers. Just let them come. Stop over-analysing, reviewing and forcing things to take shape, and let your Why come to you. It will probably hit you in the strangest of moments. And when it lands, it will make absolute perfect sense.

STEP OUT OF YOUR OWN WAY

Finding my Why was the outcome of personal development over years and years that really helped me to understand the power of surrender and detachment from outcome. I can't stress this enough: THE MOST IMPORTANT aspect for me in finding my Why has been allowing it to flow. By not trying to force or control an outcome, I've been able to truly surrender to my life's calling.

I think it's important to reiterate here that there is nothing – and I mean absolutely nothing – on the planet to demonstrate that the print magazine I launched in 2013 should have worked. Everything was stacked against us: the decline of print magazines, weakening publishing ad revenue, my complete lack of industry contacts or experience, lack of money, the fact I had only three staff members, and that I had decided to launch the first issue less than 12 months after concocting the idea. No time, no cash and no industry contacts… but I know entrepreneurs who've created magic with even less!

I could have easily blocked my own path from the start. I could have laid mental barriers in my own way. *It's too hard. Stop being ridiculous. Go back to what you're good at. Who are you to change an industry?*

But, I chose to step out of my own way and allow myself to thrive. A lot of people don't realise that our greatest enemy can be ourselves.

We once ran an article in *Collective Hub* titled 'Are You Afraid of Success?'. It got a huge amount of feedback from readers saying, "That's me!" Many entrepreneurs, creatives and highly ambitious people are guilty of holding themselves back. And too many don't even realise they're doing it! (That article is still on the *Collective Hub* website if you want to read the entire thing.) We can all be guilty of self-sabotage, of ourselves and our ventures: picking apart our own flaws, being our own worst critics, cancelling that meeting at the last minute even though it could lead to an amazing opportunity…

How have you held yourself back in the past?

Imagine yourself standing on a bridge over a river. Another version of you is standing in front of you, so you can't get by. There is your new life on the other side. You don't need to be forceful and push and shove yourself to get over there. Rather, ask this version of yourself to go with you, instead of blocking you. And then both walk across to your new life together.

You Gotta Have Faith!

I truly believe that the power of Why can unearth extraordinary and unexplainable things – even miracles! Call it faith, call it a belief in a power greater than anything tangible you can see or articulate. But I have seen again and again – in my own business and in the journeys of other visionaries – that with the right Why, grit, determination and passion, the seemingly impossible can become possible.

I know the word 'faith' is not relatable to some people. Throughout my life, I've traversed and dipped in and out of all sorts of religions, communities and belief systems, choosing to take elements of each, fascinated by certain rituals but not attaching myself to a particular one.

I don't think you have to commit to one religion to have faith. From the sweat lodges I visited in Costa Rica to ashrams in India and churches in Australia, I have walked away with lessons, strategies, mantras and memories of people I'll never forget.

And I have learnt over the years, from 'the church of entrepreneurship', that the most important belief is to have faith in yourself.

One thing I know for Sure:

There's no such thing as a 'quick fix', just as there is no 'one size fits all'. There is no pill. No guru on a rock to save you (they may offer you advice, but they can't save you). Because you have to do the work. You yourself. Your way. It's your journey. Mine was mine and I figured out what worked for me. But it's not the same for you. Only you can work that out for yourself.

CAN YOU HAVE MORE THAN ONE LOVE?

You don't necessarily need to be looking for one Why. We put Ollie Henderson on the cover of the March 2017 issue of *Collective Hub* – a fashion model/political activist/lawyer-in-training. That's a lot of slashes!

Young people are projected to have 17 jobs over 5 different careers in their lifetime. With technology changing and the rise of artificial intelligence and automation, the job of your dreams may not have even been invented yet. Who would have thought you could be a professional drone-racing driver!

My point? Don't be constrained by searching for the one great love of your working life.

If there are two industries or career paths that make you feel alive, lucky you! I know from meeting successful 'slashies' all the time that it's possible – and incredible – to have two great Whys in your world. Schoolteachers who, at night, morph into DJs; creatives who run charities; scientists who are professional sportspeople – these guys have no interest in quitting their day jobs to pursue their Why, so they live their twin purposes side by side.

Do you have Multipotentiality?

What if you love a bunch of different things and you can't figure out which direction to follow?

I love Emilie Wapnick's TED talk. Emilie is the founder of Puttylike, a home for people who have many interests and creative pursuits – AKA multipotentialites. Her talk, 'Why Some of Us Don't Have One True Calling', will be particularly helpful for anyone moving in the direction of your life's purpose with a niggling little question gnawing at you: what if I have more than *one* passion?

WORD FROM THE WHYS:
SIMON SINEK

Simon Sinek knows all about the crucial importance of finding your Why. A leadership expert and theorist who travels the globe in pursuit of his purpose – to inspire others to find their true calling – Simon describes himself as an unshakable optimist (which is, of course, another reason why I love him!). His talk on the subject – 'How Great Leaders Inspire Action' – became the third-most watched talk of all time on TED.com, notching up more than 32 million views and counting.

Better still, he's developed a smart, simple 'Why Statement' to help keep you on purpose when you find your calling.

Simon says that your Why not only expresses your unique contribution and impact, but is also a filter through which you can make decisions, every day, to act with purpose.

"Your Why Statement is one sentence that captures your unique contribution and impact," he says.

"The impact reflects the difference you want to make in the world, and the contribution is the primary action that you take towards making your impact."

your contribution

TO _____

SO THAT _____

your impact

LISA MESSENGER'S WHY:

TO

To be an entrepreneur for entrepreneurs. Living my life out loud

SO THAT

I can show others that anything is possible while living my best life.

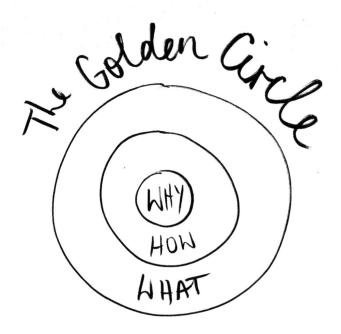

WHAT – THE OUTER LAYER

"Every person on the planet knows *What* they do. This is your job title, function, the products you sell or services you offer."

HOW – THE MIDDLE LAYER

"Some people know *How* they do it. These are the things you do that make you special, or that set you apart from your peers."

WHY – THE CORE

"Few people know *Why* they do it."

The Why is not about making money or achieving fame and fortune – that's a by-product or a result. The Why is your purpose, cause or belief. *Your Why is the very reason you exist.*

To download Simon's presentation and work through The Golden Circle for yourself, visit *startwithwhy.com/LearnYourWhy.*

What's Your Excuse?

> When people say,
> 'What should I do with my life?'
> or 'What is my life purpose?'
> what they're actually asking is this:
> 'What can I do with my time
> that is important?

— MARK MANSON

AUTHOR OF

THE SUBTLE ART OF NOT GIVING A F*CK:

A COUNTERINTUITIVE APPROACH TO LIVING A GOOD LIFE.

I recently had the good fortune of meeting Turia Pitt, an Australian ultramarathoner who survived being caught in a bush fire. We were both selected (alongside the insanely talented Indigenous Australian actress Miranda Tapsell) to feature in Disney's 'I Dare to Dream Big' campaign.

Turia suffered burns to 64 per cent of her body, has undergone nearly 200 operations and was told by doctors it was unlikely that she would ever walk again, let alone lead her old life.

Fast-forward four years and, in 2016, she completed her first Ironman triathlon. Turia has also mentored more than 6000 people through her online life-coaching programs.

What's your excuse for not reaching your full potential?

There are many things that can hold you back from finding your true purpose. Things like your upbringing and the family values you were raised with, your community and relationships, your life circumstances, your income, your career, your experience… the list goes on.

We can all probably name at least 10 factors that should or could stop us from achieving our purpose. While it's true that starting a business, travelling around the world or launching a not-for-profit is a lot easier if you have a six-figure bank balance and a bulging contact book, not having these things doesn't make it impossible. Not at all!

Ultimately, these are just excuses for living a life that is anything less than spectacular. You *deserve* spectacular! No matter what circumstances you perceive to be standing in your way, do not use them as a get-out-of-jail-free card. Don't waste your time and energy giving too much attention to people or circumstances that you can't control. Instead, work out what changes you *can* make that will have a positive impact on your life.

You have one life and one opportunity to make it count. So, don't waste it – no matter what life throws your way.

EXCUSE MYTH 1: I DON'T HAVE TIME

The facts are right there in front of us: there are 24 hours in a day, 7 days in a week, and a certain number of years in your life. We can't make more time or control how many days we have in our lives – but we *do* have control over how we use the time we have.

We know this, but all too often we don't live consistently with this belief. We waste time on things that are unimportant.

Equally, we find ourselves *experiencing* time in different ways.

Consider how long 10 minutes feels when you're stuck in bumper-to-bumper traffic. And you're running late to pick up someone from the airport. And that person happens to be your lover, who you haven't seen for weeks and you're jumping out of your skin to be reunited with them.

Does that feel like the longest 10 minutes of your life or *what*?

Now, consider how quickly 10 minutes flies by when you're engaging with someone about a topic you're both really passionate about. You might be at a meeting or chatting with a speaker after a seminar, and 10 minutes of conversation feels like 2 minutes.

In both situations, the same amount of time has passed – but our experience of that time is completely different. We can't slow time or find more of it, but we can choose to spend it consciously, powerfully and also gently (because nourishment and relaxation are as important as action).

We all have enough time to achieve anything we want in life, if we use it wisely.

EXCUSE MYTH 2: I'M TOO OLD

A woman came to our office for a book signing recently and in conversation, she casually remarked about something that happened "back when I had a career". She said it like her life was over, like there was no chance for something new or exciting to happen.

"Out of interest, how old are you?" I asked. She was 53! Hardly over the hill! The founder of the transformative TED conference series didn't even come up with his idea until he was almost 50.

This woman's best years could very well still be ahead of her. It's a matter of adopting the right attitude and perspective to put you in a positive headspace for growth and change.

EXCUSE MYTH 3: I'M NOT EXPERIENCED

This is the easiest point of all to fix. Do you know the best way to get experience? Seek out experiences! You don't even have to quit your day job to do it! These days, thanks to the Internet and the abundance of technology at your disposal, you can give yourself a crash course in your chosen industry, without even leaving your living room.

There are also amazing courses you can take to up-skill virtually. In 2016, *Collective Hub* partnered with Torrens University to launch a graduate diploma in entrepreneurship. Our students learn 'real life' industry skills from experienced industry professionals, and all of it is delivered online so they can learn whenever and wherever it suits them best.

Of course, hands-on experience does count for something. Do you know how you get hands-on experience? Seek out experiences! Sorry to repeat, but it's really that simple.

Don't do it to yourself
Don't let yourself live a small life
without higher vision or purpose.

There is a Why for you
and you're worthy of finding it
— and living it.

"What's Your Favourite Flavour of Sh*t Sandwich and Does It Come With an Olive?"

This is one of the questions best-selling author Mark Manson asked himself as he searched for his own purpose. And here's the truth he's trying to get at: everything sucks, some of the time. Nothing is ever perfect and you have to let go of the idea that, when you find your 'one thing' – your purpose, your Why – when that happens, everything in your life will suddenly fall into place and you'll run off and live happily ever after.

Spoiler alert. This is a fantasy. Everything involves hardship, challenges and difficult periods, at one stage or another.

As Mark Manson writes:

> "Everything includes some sort of cost. Nothing is pleasurable or uplifting all of the time. So the question becomes: what struggle or sacrifice are you willing to tolerate?"

It's easy to look at someone else's life – especially in the filtered age of Instagram – and glorify a profession, vocation or existence. I'm even guilty of it sometimes (in my book *Life & Love* I have a whole section on social-media perception versus reality). Of course, we take more photos of the glam dinners, cupcake deliveries and team trips to Body Barre class than we do of admin duties and stocktakes.

As Mark also writes:

> "Ultimately, what determines our ability to stick with something we care about is our ability to handle the rough patches and ride out the inevitable rotten days.
>
> "If you want to be a brilliant tech entrepreneur, but you can't handle failure, then you're not going to make it far. If you want to be a professional artist, but you aren't willing to see your work rejected hundreds, if not thousands, of times, then you're done before you start. If you want to be a hotshot court lawyer, but can't stand the 80-hour workweeks, then I've got bad news for you…"

So, think really long and hard about this:

> What unpleasant experiences are you able or willing to handle?
>
> How uncomfortable are you willing to get – physically, financially or emotionally?
>
> Are you able to pull all-nighters and give your weekends over to your passion?
>
> Do you need some big boundaries in place, so as not to affect your family, in your quest to find your Why?

Note: I've done all of the above and more… you name it, I've lived it and felt it now, in pursuit of my Why. And yes, I'd do it all again.

SUGGESTED READING TO
Inspire You.

THE DENIAL OF DEATH
by Ernest Becker

LIVING WITH INTENT
by Mallika Chopra

YOU ARE THE UNIVERSE
by Deepak Chopra and Menas Kafatos

THE ALCHEMIST
by Paulo Coelho

THRIVE
by Arianna Huffington

MY LIFE ON THE ROAD
by Gloria Steinem

THE HAPPINESS OF PURSUIT
by Chris Guillebeau

21 RITUALS TO CHANGE YOUR LIFE
by Theresa Cheung

THE NEW OLD ME
by Meredith Maran

THE RULES DO NOT APPLY
by Ariel Levy

EYES WIDE OPEN
by Isaac Lidsky

RAPT: ATTENTION AND THE FOCUSED LIFE
by Winifred Gallagher

THE WANDER SOCIETY
by Keri Smith

THE ART OF TRAVEL
by Alain de Botton

ORIGINALS
by Adam Grant

EAT PRAY LOVE MADE ME DO IT
by Elizabeth Gilbert

THE BOOK OF JOY
by the Dalai Lama, Desmond Tutu and Douglas Carlton Abrams

THE SUBTLE ART OF NOT GIVING A F*CK
by Mark Manson

BIG MAGIC
by Elizabeth Gilbert

THE HAPPINESS PROJECT
by Gretchen Rubin

WHITE HOT TRUTH
by Danielle LaPorte

100 THINGS: WHAT'S ON YOUR LIST?
by Sebastian Terry

START WITH WHY
by Simon Sinek

When I stopped caring about what other people thought about me.

I truly stepped into my greatness zone.

Just Say YES!

One of my philosophies in life is that, when an opportunity presents itself that aligns with my Why, I jump into it 1 million per cent. Pronto. Without delay.

A recent example of this was the opportunity to interview the incredibly talented and inspirational Danielle LaPorte, an entrepreneur and international speaker from Canada.

Danielle was in Australia for only a short time and the window of opportunity to speak to her was whisper thin. Unfortunately, that whisper-thin window happened to collide with me returning from an overseas trip.

To squeeze the interview in, I would have to come out of an intense program at a retreat in India, drive five hours to the airport, sleep in a hotel from midnight until 5am, catch a plane at 7am (with a four-hour stopover in Bangkok), arrive in Sydney, walk off the plane into a waiting car that would drive me straight to hair and make-up, get camera-ready, then arrive fresh-faced to my meeting with Danielle, ready to chat with her on behalf of our *Collective Hub* community.

Or, I could handball the interview to one of the amazing writers at *Collective Hub*.

Can you guess which option I took?

If you flick over to the next page, you'll see I connected so well with Danielle that I wound up asking her to share some pearls of wisdom in this book!

It's not that our senior writers at *Collective Hub* couldn't have handled the interview – they would have done a brilliant job. But this is an example, pure and simple, of me living my Why. I was exhausted when I met Danielle, and truth be told, I would have loved nothing more than to collapse into bed and sleep. But my Why is to be an entrepreneur for entrepreneurs, living my life out loud, showing people that anything is possible.

Meeting and connecting with peers like Danielle is core to my purpose, and if I can't sacrifice a little sleep and comfort to make an interview like this happen – one that could generate incredible insights and aha moments for our community – then what is the point of all of this?

When you go down this path and start really, deeply connecting with your Why and your life's purpose, you'll make this discovery for yourself, too.

It's not always easy.

In fact, sometimes it's downright difficult and exponentially exhausting, and you'll ask yourself over and over again: is this *really* worth it?

The answer? It is. One billion times over, it is.

WORD FROM THE WHYS:
DANIELLE LAPORTE

A self-confessed introvert who hated inserting herself into conversations, Danielle LaPorte could have chosen a career that allowed her to shrink into the background. But, driven by her Why, the author, entrepreneur and former think-tank executive now runs a self-development empire dedicated to helping people live their fullest lives. Struggling to find your true purpose? Here's Danielle's advice:

Ask yourself one question…

WHAT HAS TO DIE FOR YOU
TO LIVE YOUR WHY?

"Women and feminine-identified types specialise in beginnings, not endings. We prefer to nurture, not exclude. This, of course, is spectacular and divine and… challenging. Because destruction is essential to creation. Something has to die for your dream to be born. And by that I mean… you may need to cut off its life or air supply and send it down the river to die."

What in your life has to die so that *you* can be the change?

Danielle suggests that you:

Stop feeding your doubts. Step away from questionable news sources and social-media gorging.

Cut off the air supply to panic and despair.
Panic is never, ever useful. Not ever.

Cut cords with depressing thoughts. This is a spiritual practice. "Thank you [God, Universe or your preferred deity] for cutting cords with thoughts and energies that are not aligned with my highest Truth and Joy." This is great to do before you go to sleep.

Stop giving Scooby snacks (AKA *attention*) to trolls and haters. They feed on it. Don't feed them.

Leave your fear of judgment in the sun to melt. Melt the fear of being called inexperienced, flighty, feminist, angry, divisive, airy-fairy, delusional, too inclusive, too young, too old, too soft, too hard, too loud…

Take your family karma off life support. You don't need to play small because you don't want to out-earn, out-shine or out-politic your parents. Let the karma die, so you can keep the love alive.

Smother your addiction to chaos. With an even greater desire for peace and simplicity.

Let the limitations die. Those old thought forms will put up a fight. You will be tempted to give them your time and nourishment because you're an innately loving creature. But don't. Instead, water the dream; weed out the energy-pests.

YOU'RE GOING TO FAIL.
IT'S GUARANTEED.

IT'S GOING TO HAPPEN EVENTUALLY
IF IT HASN'T HAPPENED ALREADY,
AND YOU WILL NOT MEET ONE SINGLE
IN-LOVE, VIBRANT, FISCALLY THRIVING,
SUCCESSFUL-ON-THEIR-OWN-TERMS
PERSON WHO HAS NOT FAILED.

IT'S AN INITIATION: WHAT DOESN'T
KILL YOU MAKES YOU STRONGER.
SO JUST PICK ONE OF THE FIVE
THINGS YOU'VE BEEN NOODLING
OVER AT THE MOMENT,
AND JUST DO IT.

– Danielle LaPorte

This Big Life

If I could tell you the fastest way to find your Why and discover your meaning for being put on this planet, you'd want to know the answer – right? Of course you would – that's why you picked up this book!

Okay then, I'm going to let you in on a little secret. To do so, I'm going to talk about Canadian miners, tantric sex and severed toes. Bear with me!

Nowadays I have a big life and it's really busy, stupidly easy to get disconnected. I can become separated from real, present conversations and get distanced from intimate, connected relationships, which is the last place I want to be.

My public life is surreal to me. I can be on stage and have 1000 people screaming at me and lining up afterwards to take a selfie and request my autograph – it's incredibly humbling. I love meeting our community when I'm on the road and presenting, so these experiences always make me pinch myself.

But the flip side is that it can be such a disconnected existence at times. Racing around to catch flights, presenting in four cities in one week, squeezing in meetings and dinners and catch-ups between it all – it's crazy busy. Just check out a sample of my week on the right to get a taste.

My life in seven days

People often ask me what a week in the life of Lisa looks like. Well, there are no formulaic weeks, which keeps it fresh and interesting, but impossible to share a standard schedule. So here is the week I've just had, at the time of writing, to give you an example of just how varied it gets with my different hats and roles: swinging between CEO and editor, speaker and entrepreneur, influencer to daughter to partner to friend.

MONDAY

7am: Hair and make-up for Swarovski photoshoot for their Mother's Day campaign with Mama

8.30–11am: Shoot photo and video series for the campaign (what an honour and delight to do it with Mum!)

11.30am: Discuss next three *Collective Hub* magazine covers with our editor

12.30pm: Meet with head of my advisory board to talk next three months' strategy

1.15pm: Barre class, then quick bite to eat

2.30pm: Advertising client meeting to discuss upcoming brief and strategise a kick-arse campaign

3.30pm: Debrief with my partnerships team

4pm: Some time writing this book...

5pm: Leave office early to go for a walk – Bondi to Bronte with Mum

6.30pm: Big shop-up to cook a yummy meal with Mama (cooking is one of my all-time fave things to do to unwind)

TUESDAY

7am: 1-hour guided meditation at home, then drop Mum at airport

9.15am: Daily content meeting with my digital team (side note: we do up to 240 stories a month now on collectivehub.com)

9.45am: General team catch-ups, strategic check-ins and bout of emails

1–3pm: Nestlé Purina workshop on intrapreneurship, disruption and staying relevant for their Australian & NZ marketing teams

3.30pm: Phone call with major CEO on potential strategic partnership

5.30pm: Speaking gig: Y Connect (YWCA) Twilight Seminar Series at CBA Innovation Lab – 'Women Who Shaped the Industry' for YWCA programs and services helping women and children escape domestic and family violence

8pm: Show at Sydney Opera House with a friend

10pm: Fall into bed exhausted

WEDNESDAY

8am: Speaking gig: Connected Women Australia & NZ Panel at Facebook HQ for International Women's Day

11am: Meet media agency with my head of partnerships

12.15pm: Barre class

2pm: Pre-record radio interview for International Women's Day

3pm: Write article for *Forbes*

4pm: Internal team meeting re: upcoming *Collective Hub* 101 Masterclass series

5pm: Cash flow and P&L meeting with our financial controller

6–7pm: Visioning a community extension for *Collective Hub* that I am keen to build

8pm: Home, quick dinner and flop into bed

THURSDAY

Morning at home:
Meditating, journaling, writing my next editor's letter and Bondi-to-Bronte walk and swim with Benny my dog (sometimes I work from home to power through and have some 'me' time)

Noon: Speaking gig: CPA Australia International Women's Day Lunch at Ivy Ballroom, speaking on a panel

3pm: Interview with *HuffPost* for two upcoming articles

3.30pm: Internal meeting on our upcoming Kick Start Smart conference

4pm: Client advertising pitch meeting

5pm: Hair and make-up for *Beauty & The Beast* Australian movie premiere

6pm: Red carpet arrivals (I took my fab PA, Georgia, to this one. I always try to take different members of my team to events, to reward them and to spend one-on-one time with them)

10pm: Super late snack at Fratelli Paradiso in Potts Point

11.30pm: Bed

FRIDAY

7am: Skype call to LA to chat about next month's cover of *Collective Hub* magazine

9.15am: Daily content meeting (clearly, with my schedule I don't make them all!)

10am: Weekly catch-ups with each of my management team

11.30am: Lexus planning meeting (we have an incredible campaign going on with them for start-ups)

1pm: Mentoring session with one of my mentees

2pm: Writing and general email catch-ups

4pm: Drinks with my team to celebrate another big week

5pm: Leave to meet friends and head to the Adele concert (she was incredible!)

SATURDAY

Morning: Finally! A relaxing morning at home to chill out and reset.

Evening: A Moveable Feast dinner on Bondi Beach, barefoot and dancing the night away with friends.

SUNDAY

All day: Writing this book!

This is why, for me, it's so important to be as present and conscious as possible in every single moment of my day. To connect. To really *be there*. Even if I'm just catching a taxi or an Uber... because this is where moments of pure gold can happen.

For instance, when I was in the cab on my way to the airport on a recent trip, I had one of the most extraordinary conversations of my life because I was connected and present. Most people jump into a cab and switch off – or more accurately, switch on to their devices and social media – but I tucked my phone away and got chatting with the driver.

"I'm off to LA!" I said excitedly. "Have you been anywhere interesting recently?"

The driver told me that his last trip was at Christmas-time. He flew to America to catch up with a childhood friend. He had grown up in Jerusalem with this friend before they both moved with their families to different continents: he to Australia, his friend to America.

"I searched for him for years and years, and finally, after 31 years I found him," the driver told me. "I flew to America and got to spend Christmas with him and his family. When I arrived, there were 200 people from his family and community there to welcome me!"

I was mesmerised by this story; can you imagine reconnecting with a friend from childhood and being welcomed in such an extraordinary way? It gave me goosebumps! And it put me in a fantastic mood as I prepared for a lengthy 13hr+ plane ride.

It was such a simple, yet life-affirming conversation. And I would have totally missed it if I'd played on my phone.

Drawing from Extraordinary Life Lessons

But back to tantric sex. And miners in Canada. And severed toes…

I'm not sure about you, but I have very little experience with the tantric arts. So when I happened across a tantric pulsation workshop in the foothills of India, during my pilgrimage to the East early in 2017, I signed up for the five-day workshop.

This harks back to my philosophy to lean into discomfort. When I see something that intrigues or challenges me, that I don't understand and that makes me uncomfortable, I'll dive right in – even if I'm sh*t scared about what might happen along the way!

So I thought, "Why not?" The day before the course, I bumped into one of my new friends, Hamish – a giant bear of a man. He hails from Northwest Canada, where he's been a miner for 30 years.

"Lisa!" he bellowed. "I saw your name on the tantric workshop and I signed up, too!"

Hamish, as I would go on to learn during this workshop, is absolutely hilarious. He's this big, gruff-looking guy with a penchant for blowing up cars at weddings, who works in sub-zero conditions in Canadian mines. He's probably not someone

I would cross paths with in my everyday life, yet somehow, by day two of the workshop, we were the best of friends.

He had been travelling to India for 25 years and heard about the commune, so decided to come along and explore it. And that's how I found myself becoming close friends with a man from a different world – geographically and pretty much in every other sense of the word – because both of us were on the same path of seeking and being unafraid to push ourselves further.

That's what I love about stepping into strange situations; you never know where, or to whom, it might lead you.

And you know the funny thing about the tantric workshop we went to? It had absolutely nothing to do with sex! Instead, it challenged us to deconstruct our judgments and existing beliefs, and it prompted loads of interesting conversations and revelations.

In our group sessions, Hamish shared that he was going through a difficult divorce. The next minute, he was talking about how the local bar in his hometown keeps a jar of toes. *Human toes.* Our conversations were diverse, shocking, stunning and eye opening. Aren't these the kind of experiences we should live for?

HOW TO OPEN YOUR OWN EYES

It doesn't have to be some weird workshop in India that gets you out of the ordinary and puts you in situations where you can learn from people you wouldn't normally meet.

It could be listening to music you don't normally listen to, or going to places you don't normally go. Saying 'yes' to the invitation your gut instinct would normally turn down – the loud rock concert, or the intimate dinner with a casual acquaintance.

The next time you're sitting in a café, put your phone down, make eye contact and interact with people. That's one of the best things about having a dog – strangers actually stop and chat with you.

At the moment, after moving to a new area, I've committed to doing one thing a week locally that I've never done before. It could be something as simple as eating in a new restaurant, playing tennis against two eight-year-olds (they beat me!), walking a different route to the office or spending my lunchbreak at a bookshop, in a section that I'd normally walk past.

Seek creative outlets. Try different hobbies. Interact with people you don't normally hang out with and don't be afraid to put yourself out there. Breathe, paint, draw, colour, cook, read, sing, stretch, knit, craft, build, code, deep-dive, research, meditate... do it all. And then some. Soon, your real passions in life will start to reveal themselves to you.

Do something that pushes you in a different direction, challenges your norm and saturates your soul with new experiences, information or feelings. You never know what ideas it might trigger – and what fun you'll have along the way.

How can I leave my mark on the world, I thought, unless I get out there first and see it?

– PHIL KNIGHT

Embracing Aloneness

For any of you who are familiar with my writing and *Collective Hub*, you'll know I only ever write from my personal experience and my learnings. And I always write from right where I am in that very moment, boots and all. Raw and real. Unapologetically.

That's why I want to share with you my recent experiences with aloneness. In the past six months or so, I've done a deep dive into some pretty intense self-exploration… It's been brave. It's been courageous. It's been pretty crazy. I haven't explored this level of self-inquiry for some years, and it has brought me huge awareness around the notion of 'aloneness' and what this truly means.

I think there is *so much stigma* attached to the notion of being alone. In my experience, there are certain times that trigger each of us and send us into feelings of abandonment, fear and the perception that we're not good enough.

A perfect example of this is Valentine's Day. It's one day of hyped-up romance, love and connection that acts as a trigger for many – and trust me, I get it, as I have also been in that space.

Recently however, I've spent a lot of time consciously choosing to be alone – just me and my monkey mind – and also in complete emptiness. Contrary to what you may think, when I'm home in Sydney I spend a great deal of time alone. I absolutely love it – now. In my twenties? Not so much. I hated being alone with myself and my miserable thoughts.

But now, being alone is something that I'm perfectly okay with – I'm *more* than okay with it. I lead an increasingly public life, thanks to you guys. It's what I've chosen to step into, and not a moment goes by that I'm not exceptionally grateful for it. Yet, the flip side of that coin is that I need downtime to recalibrate. I recharge by being in my own company (or that of my partner or very close friends).

I love one-on-one time and I relish the very, very simple things in life – meditation, cooking, yoga, dog walks, travel, writing, sitting in the sunshine. I avoid planning weekends and love to be spontaneous as much as possible.

Why am I talking about this? Because so often, people are not okay with aloneness. And we should be – being alone is absolutely nothing to be ashamed about. To get really raw and existential (and to paraphrase Osho): we are born alone and we die alone. In between those two moments in time, we scramble around trying to accumulate relationships, families, loves, careers and hobbies to fill our time and give us purpose. But the truth of the matter is that we are ultimately alone. Rather than trying to escape from aloneness, why not learn to tolerate it, enjoy it and even rejoice in it? It's from this space of stillness that we can go within and ultimately get stronger on our own, to step into our Why and take it out to the broader world.

When you truly embrace aloneness you never need to feel lonely again.

You come home,
make some tea,
sit down in an armchair
and all around there is silence.

Everyone decides for themselves
whether that's loneliness
or freedom.

– UNKNOWN

You
must get
comfortable

with feeling uncomfortable.

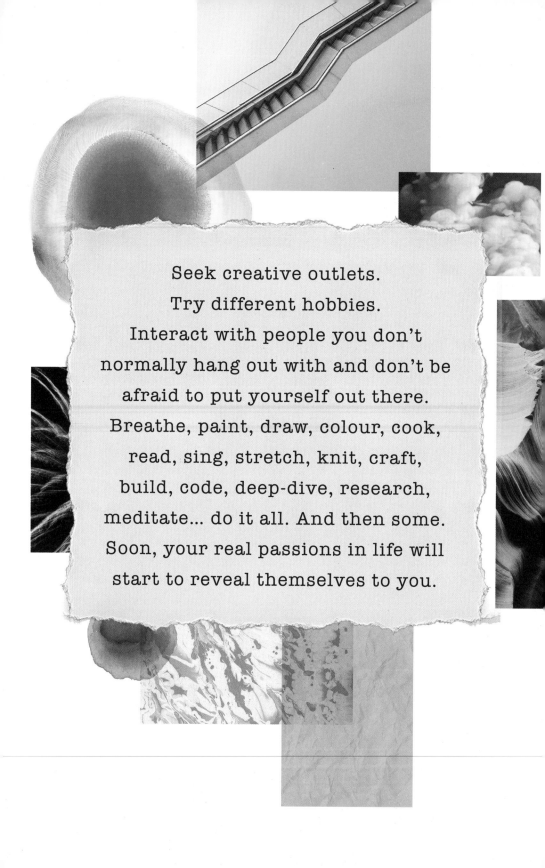

Seek creative outlets.
Try different hobbies.
Interact with people you don't
normally hang out with and don't be
afraid to put yourself out there.
Breathe, paint, draw, colour, cook,
read, sing, stretch, knit, craft,
build, code, deep-dive, research,
meditate... do it all. And then some.
Soon, your real passions in life will
start to reveal themselves to you.

Stepping Into Your Why

To get ready to tune into your purpose, it helps to drown out the noise from other sources so you can focus on finding your inner drive. Go blank on social media for a few days while you do this internal work. Instead of checking out what's happening online, check in to what's happening with you.

As I've touched on earlier, when you're trying to find your Why you can be so eager that you almost force it, looking for outcomes that aren't there. To stay in flow and on the right track, try to listen for consistent statements the people around you make about you.

You may have natural talents that you take for granted and dabble in part-time – could there be a way to elevate them from hobby to career? People often see things in us that we don't recognise in ourselves, so think for a moment: what are the things you do naturally, unconsciously, without even putting in much effort that people compliment you on? The things you're good at, which come easily?

Determine How You Measure Your Life

How do we possibly measure success and happiness, when their very definition is going to be so different for each one of us? I'm not talking about success in relation to material trappings – the beautiful inspiring home, the fast sports cars and fancy yachts, the designer clothes, movie-star friends, front-row seats and VIP lifestyle…

All of that stuff can be amazing, but they are by-products of a purpose-led life. To really live according to your Why, you need to connect to something much deeper than the pursuit of trinkets and toys.

A little while ago I discussed the concept of defining and measuring happiness with futurist and philosopher Jason Silva. This is what he shared:

"I think the role of sentience, of self-awareness, of consciousness, is that we can actually be the canvas and the paintbrush *and* the paint. We get to impregnate the world with *meaning*. The ability to create a sense of volition and agency and purpose in our life; this is what characterises us as meaning-making and meaning-seeking creatures.

"The only way forwards is to use our wherewithal and our genius to remake the rules and reset the terms. We have done beautifully well so far as a society. For instance, we didn't evolve to fly, yet we incorporate non-biological props and we can now fly aircrafts across the sky. We didn't evolve to be telepathic, yet devices made of plastic and metal in our pockets allow us to share our thoughts telepathically across the planet.

"Oh! Universe, you didn't hand us these terms? Well, we are gonna go and create them. Because we *are* the Universe."

MONEY AND MEANING

"Many people want to create a start-up and be the next Mark Zuckerberg and become a billionaire. But here's something to ponder: one thing that we know about money and fame is that they don't heal," says Jason.

That doesn't mean we don't need money. I wrote an entire book on this subject, *Money & Mindfulness*, which explores self-worth and money as a means to reach your higher purpose.

"Having resources *helps*," says Jason. "Money facilitates the movement of resources towards expanding your sense of volition and agency in the world. But having money of and in itself is not the end all, at all, at all.

"So: perhaps we should redefine what it means to be a billionaire – to extend it beyond money? A billion dollars makes you a billionaire. But much more interesting to me is a billionaire who can positively affect the lives of a billion people. If you make a video that gets a billion views, that makes a billion people smile, you're a billionaire to me," he says.

It is in our self-interest to develop a sense of purpose and to conjure up a passion. It will govern our actions in the world – and those actions will create real results in the real world.

– JASON SILVA

HOW GENEROUS DO YOU WANT TO BE?

A big part of many people's Why is being able to give back. And yes, I do mean financially. Whether it's donating a percentage of your profits to charity, investing in other start-ups or paying for employees to attend conferences or extracurricular self-development courses, one of the amazing side effects of running a profitable business is that you have resources at hand that you can use to empower others.

On an extreme scale, the most incredible example of this is The Giving Pledge, which was started by Warren Buffet and Bill and Melinda Gates. It's a public commitment by the world's wealthiest individuals and families to dedicate the majority of their wealth to philanthropy. Other entrepreneurs choose to set up their own not-for-profit arms, such as Mark Zuckerberg and Priscilla Chan's philanthropic organisation, which aims to invest US$3 billion to eradicate disease.

Of course, we don't all have billions in the bank, but consider how you can integrate generosity into your purpose, at a small level. It can be difficult when you're on a shoestring, but studies show that giving back boosts morale, eases anxiety, fights depression and enhances a person's sense of purpose. What can you give away?

Balance Commercial with Creative

In finding and living your purpose, you need to have a certain amount of commercial acumen about you. Yes, you want to be able to do what you love each day, but you also have to draw a fine balance between passion projects and paying the bills.

Artists, for instance, may love creating a certain aesthetic on the canvas, but find there's actually no market for what they love to paint. Ken Done is an extraordinary artist, but what he loved painting and what became commercially successful for him were two very different things. Ken was painting all sorts of incredible pieces before he painted a koala, but became globally known as the artist who painted koalas and the Sydney Opera House on Sheridan sheets! Yet, having that commercial side enabled him to keep doing what he loves with his art. My good friend David Bromley is similar, and one of the most commercial and brilliant artists I know.

Balancing the commercial and the creative is tangibly linked, like two sides of a coin. Money makes the world go around, obviously, but you don't want to damage your reputation by hawking a business that doesn't align with your values.

For me personally, no amount of money on the planet right now could convince me to bastardise my brand. It takes 20 years to build a brand of substance, and just 20 minutes to tear it down.

Reach a State of Surrender

The magic happens when
we're in flow – free, open, aware,
in the moment, intentional, willing.
Don't fall into the trap of the masses
by skipping ahead and forcing
your world to submit. It won't.

For many people who are striving towards a goal or a set outcome, the idea of surrendering is akin to giving up. But that's not what I mean – far from it.

I'm referring to the act of letting go of your *perception of control*. Because honestly, that's all it is – a perception – and the truth of the matter is that when you force anything too hard, it often falls apart under pressure.

Eiman Al Zaabi, author of *The Art of Surrender: A Practical Guide to Enlightened Happiness and Well-Being*, explains that our duty lies "not in controlling our lives, but in being able to sit within ourselves and develop a deeper understanding of the self's desires." In this way we can develop a deeper understanding of our desires, our vision and our ability to create good and make an impact in the world.

"There is a future story that wants to be told through your life," says Eiman. "This story needs to be listened to, and when you do listen, life takes on a different meaning. You begin to move in unity with your purpose."

Trying to force an outcome is completely counterintuitive. Even though you are desperate, even though you're itching for things to change, even though you're so ready to move into your purpose that even one more day of waiting seems unbearable… even then, you need patience.

Because when you surrender, you are quite literally falling into 'flow' – my favourite state of being.

I've also been reading *The Surrender Experiment: My Journey into Life's Perfection* by Michael Singer, which has some good themes you might want to explore. And *The Untethered Soul: The Journey Beyond Yourself* is extraordinary!

Surrender is such an important part of the journey of discovering your Why. I unequivocally believe that I have only been able to achieve my level of success by being in flow – when it works, when I'm totally in flow and not forcing or trying to control an outcome, this is when the magic happens.

Honestly, you need to feel this.

If what we do for a living stems from who we truly are – our values, our beliefs – we will always be in the right place to achieve greatness.

For example, at *Collective Hub* we are all about igniting human potential.

For every opportunity that comes our way, I ask: does that ignite human potential? It's our litmus test. If someone wants to do a fashion label with our brand, does that ignite human potential? No, it doesn't. What about starting a university course to educate entrepreneurs, does that ignite human potential? Hell yes!

Now, did I set out with the goal of creating a university course? Not a chance. But by adopting a Zen-like nature, staying in flow and being open to opportunities, it enables things to come to me and pass through me.

Of course, we have certain strategic plans and goals. But I never try to force an outcome that is not naturally brewing. For me, it's all about energy and flow and being open, rather than ticking items off a list and moving in a certain direction because it's on a business plan.

Surrendering to this process is key. What this means is that all day, every day when you're open, people want to collaborate, share, grow and partner with you – and there are boundless opportunities to create beyond your wildest dreams.

CONTROL $\longrightarrow$ AGGRESSIVE, MASCULINE, HARD ENERGY

FLOW $\longrightarrow$ INSPIRING, CREATIVE, SOFT ENERGY

PURPOSE

A purpose-led life is a blessed life.

— DR ROBERT HOLDEN

QUIZ
Are You Living Your Why?

It's not about what you do, but why you do it. Living your Why in your working life means finding the sweet spot between what you care about, what lights you up, what makes you 'you' and, potentially, connecting with something greater than yourself.

Your Why comprises several elements – your values, your passion, your impact and your authenticity. You need to be satisfying all four elements to be living your Why. Want to know how you're tracking? Have a think about what each of these four categories entails in your life, then follow the prompts below – it's time for a stocktake.

TICK EACH STATEMENT THAT RINGS TRUE FOR YOU.

IF YOU TICK AT LEAST 2 OUT OF 3 POINTS FOR AN ELEMENT, COLOUR IT IN ON YOUR VISUAL WHY CHECK-UP

VALUES

Your values could be health, finances, family and friends, creativity, social responsibility, the environment, a flexible lifestyle… you name it.

☐ I prioritise what is important to me.

☐ My work allows space for what I value.

☐ My work aligns with my values.

PASSION

Is writing your thing? Do numbers float your boat? Or can you not go a week without trying the latest dessert?

☐ My friends say I light up when I talk about work.

☐ If money were no object, I would keep doing what I'm doing.

☐ At least one thing I am good at and enjoy doing features in my job description.

IMPACT

Your impact could be anything from changing the world to brightening the day of that customer you served with a smile.

- ☐ I'm contributing to a company or cause I care about (beyond my bank account).

- ☐ What I do benefits the life of at least one other person.

- ☐ I am changing a small patch of the world in some way via my work.

AUTHENTICITY

You, yes you, without the mask.

- ☐ I am being unapologetically me at work.

- ☐ I have consciously chosen this path rather than trying to satisfy others' expectations.

- ☐ I can truly find enjoyment in my job, rather than _____.

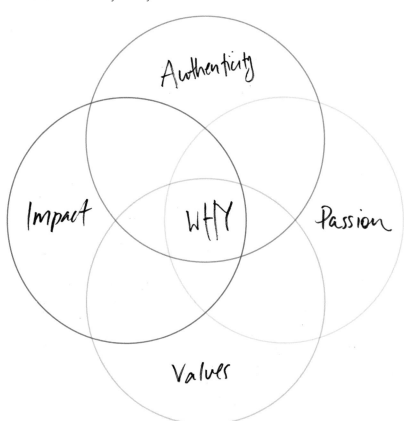

DECODING YOUR RESULTS

Not living your Why? It's time to focus on how you can strengthen the areas
that are holding you back. If your answers made it clear that your work doesn't
nurture one area, whether it's your values, passion, impact or authenticity
(or all four!), it's time to take action.

VALUES

First up, identify your values. What areas of your life guide your decision-making?
Do you shape your life around travel, personal growth, wealth, relationships,
freedom, changing the world? How can you start to make your working life
incorporate these priorities?

PASSION

Not sure of your passion? What do you think about, talk about, do in your
downtime? What gets you out of bed in the morning (it could even be dashing
to read the news headlines, hear your favourite podcast, or leaping out for a daily
run)? Grab your pen and paper, talk to the people who know you best and be
brutally honest with yourself.

IMPACT

What sort of impact would you most like to make on the world? What causes are
close to your heart – is it social inequality, animal welfare, the environment? Once
you've identified the area in which you'd most like to make a difference, can you
integrate it into your current job – or can you envision a role where you could?

AUTHENTICITY

Not being true to yourself in your working life? Could it be out of fear, or a
reluctance to step out of your comfort zone? Identify the belief that's holding
you back from being your authentic self, for example, "I'm scared I'll fail." Now
flip that fear around and reframe it: "I'm so excited to succeed." Write this on a
Post-it and stick it somewhere you'll see it every day to motivate you to show up
as – and only for a gig that allows you to be – your true self.

The scariest thing imaginable would be not to live your best life.

HOW'S THAT EGO OF YOURS GOING?

Your purpose is bigger than your ego – the voice in your head telling you that you are separate from everyone else. Your ego makes your purpose all about feeling special, unique, superior and less neurotic than others. DROP THIS. This is the wrong path to take. Your ego has no place here. Remember where you came from and *never* take it for granted.

5 QUICK STEPS TO KEEP YOUR EGO IN CHECK

ONE
Understand the difference between healthy self-esteem and ego. There are many people in positions of power that have a scary balance of low self-esteem and big ego. This is a recipe for disaster.

TWO
Consider the inherent impermanence of all things – what is of monumental importance today is probably relatively trivial shortly after.

THREE
Think about your size in proportion to the Universe as a whole – this is a humbling exercise.

FOUR
Accept praise but never depend on it. Become desensitised to overzealous bolstering and, instead, listen carefully to those closest to you for a humbling reality check.

FIVE
Take time to reflect on your shortcomings, and take responsibility and learn from mistakes. Be open to continuous improvement to become the very best version of you.

WORD FROM THE WHYS:
LEWIS HOWES

When I finally achieved
my dream, I felt empty.

Entrepreneur, former professional American football player and host of podcast talk show 'The School of Greatness' Lewis Howes has learnt what it's like to get everything you ever wanted in life – only to realise that a life without purpose is miserable, regardless of how big your bank balance is. As a long-time supporter of *Collective Hub,* he and I follow each other's journeys and champion each other's passions. Here's what Lewis has to say about purpose:

> "Since I was a kid, I've been obsessed with how to create greatness. In sports, in business, in relationships, in impact.

> "I set my sights on becoming an All-American athlete and did everything I could to get there. But when I finally achieved my dream, I felt empty. Disappointed. Angry. Frustrated. Just sad.

"I kept going, thinking that becoming a pro-football player would be fulfilling.

"And it was, for a minute – until I got injured in my rookie season and couldn't return to the sport after major surgery.

"Then I felt *really* empty. *Really* disappointed. *Really* frustrated.

"I couldn't shake my need to chase greatness but I had no clue how to go about it at that point. So I started over and, slowly but surely, I built a business that made millions.

"Yet again, I felt a sense of emptiness. I had money and success now, but I still wasn't living my full purpose.

"And then something shifted that led me to a whole new way of living.

"I started a podcast with the purpose of being of service to others. I wanted to share what I was learning from the amazing people in my life with a larger audience.

"Something amazing started to happen: I felt a level of purpose come into my life that I'd been seeking for years.

"The more positive, helpful, inspiring conversations I shared with the world, the more people sent me messages about how they were being impacted by the messages.

"The more messages I got, the more motivation I had to make better episodes, reach more people, and become a better interviewer.

"Fast-forward four years and I've never been more fulfilled or certain that I'm living my life's purpose.

"The impact of shifting my career to be in service to others, versus in service to myself and my bank account, is priceless. I now know that a life of purpose is one that is focused on service to others through your own unique talents and abilities.

"It's about giving and giving and giving some more.

"And it's about being grateful for every opportunity to serve – no matter how small or large."

Everyone Has the Chance to Change

It's hard to get out of the barrel.
It's slippery around the edges
and people are happy to see you fall back in.

— ROBERT DOWNEY JNR

I've borrowed these words from Robert, the king of comebacks if ever there was one! He moved past a drug addiction, a jail sentence and career troubles and somehow leveraged his second chance to become one of Hollywood's most sought-after actors. If Robert doesn't embody second chances and successful comebacks, I don't know who does.

Still, he isn't the only person to have failed – once, twice or dozens of times. Neither is he the only person who has brilliantly turned his life around. Every one of us has the chance to change our actions and our feelings.

We only get one life, but that doesn't mean we only get one opportunity. Potential, hope and possibility abound: it's up to you to see where they take you.

FOUR SUCCESSFUL PEOPLE
WHOSE WHY CHANGED THEIR LIVES

MARTHA STEWART

Martha worked as a full-time model to put herself through university and later as a Wall Street stockbroker before she morphed into the domestic goddess and cupcake guru we now know. This move has earned her a reported US$400 million fortune.

"This is what truly interests us, why we all come to work every day ... our passion is and always should be to make life better," says Martha of her empire.

Martha developed a taste for cooking during her career as a banker. She used to entertain clients at some of New York's top restaurants and ask the chefs to share their secrets. The rest is history...

SARA BLAKELY

Sara sold office supplies door-to-door before launching the underwear brand that made her the US's youngest self-made female billionaire. The founder of Spanx was famously inspired to create the slimming pants when she couldn't find underwear to wear under white jeans.

But her purpose is bigger than that. The Sara Blakely Foundation supports charities that empower women.

"Before starting Spanx, I wrote in my journal that I wanted to invent a product that would make millions of women feel good," she says.

JEFF BEZOS

Jeff wanted to be a space explorer when he was a child but went into banking, becoming the youngest-ever senior vice president at hedge fund firm D.E. Shaw. It was there that he found his true purpose.

While researching the growth of the world wide web, he discovered it had grown 2300% in one year and saw an opportunity. He made a list of 20 possible categories to sell online, before settling on books. In the first month of its launch, Amazon had sold books to people in all 50 US states and in 45 different countries.

The Amazon Why? "To be Earth's most customer centric-company; to build a place where people can come to find and discover anything they might want to buy online."

Today, Jeff also owns a space exploration company called Blue Origin.

DREW BARRYMORE

Drew, one of *Collective Hub's* most popular cover stars, hasn't totally turned her back on acting but is now a 'slashie', combining TV roles with directing and executive producing, and running her own beauty company.

After a lifetime spent on set in make-up artists' chairs, she was inspired to launch Flower Beauty, a cosmetics company that aims to empower women by not selling them an unrealistic ideal of beauty.

STOP.
HEART
CHECK

Ask yourself WHY
about every activity on this day.
If you're content with the answer,
carry on.

If not,
be courageous
and
brave enough
to correct
your course.

part 3.

WHAT

TO DO WITH YOUR WHY

Anything Is Possible When You Find Your Why

Since launching *Collective Hub*, I've been lucky enough to sit in on the Page One editorial meeting at the *New York Times* – twice. I've spent an hour with iconic *Vogue* editor Anna Wintour, in a one-on-one meeting at her request. I've been personally invited to Sir Richard Branson's private getaway, Necker Island, and to his private island Makepeace in Australia. I've met dozens of interesting, innovative, creative people who happen to be wildly famous. I've sat front row at fashion shows, I've signed an international book deal and I've done so, so, *so* many other things that I once believed were well beyond my wildest dreams…

And all of this has been possible for one reason, and one reason only: I found my Why. Then I went out and lived it. I lived it big! And loud. Proud. Bold. Confronting. Uncomfortable. Stressful. Stress-free.

There are days when it all seems too hard, and days when I feel so ridiculously blessed, positive, grateful and humble. But on both kinds of days, I'm living my Why unquestionably. Resolutely. Fully.

Because I know that when you're in the space of living your Why, the sky is the limit. Or as I prefer to say, there is absolutely no limit at all. Who knows for sure what is beyond your sky…

PURPOSE

2012 ⇝ 2013

OUR FIRST ISSUE
HITS NEWSSTANDS
ACROSS 5000 OUTLETS.
PROUD MOMENT! ↳

Launch issue featuring cover
star Lorna Jane Clarkson
(who just so happens to
be in this book). ↘

Ewan McGregor interview.

Amazing to have been one
of the few media outlets to
get a one-on-one!

BIG DREAMS
AND WHERE IT
ALL BEGAN!

2014

The launch of
*Daring & Disruptive:
Unleashing The
Entrepreneur*
– the book that kicked
off this whole series!

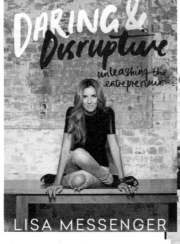

COLLECTIVE HUB TURNS ONE!

THIS SHOT WAS TAKEN AT THE LAUNCH PARTY.

MAKING SOCIAL MEDIA MILESTONES ☺

WOW

10K followers

thanks for believing in me xx

Being invited to
meet Bill Clinton.

Hanging out with Sir Richard
Branson on Necker Island.
This has been one of the most
incredible highlights to date.

A wonderful meeting with
nna Wintour at *Vogue* HQ in NYC.
This trip was extraordinary and
ushed me unlike anything before.

Daring & Disruptive
published in the USA!!

JODIE O'SHEA
ORPHANAGE
IN INDONESIA.
THE MOST PRECIOUS
WAY TO CLOSE
OFF 2012

A shot my mum took of the
High Line in NYC.

his trip included the biggest
nd most impactful meetings
of my life with some
serious global players!

2015: the year of two more books
and playbooks – *Money &
Mindfulness* and *Life & Love*.

AMAZING MOMENT
IN THE MIMCO MOTHER'S DAY
CAMPAIGN WITH MAMA X

2016

Canberra Trip: MALCOLM TURNBULL AND WYATT ROY

we ♥ all 100K of you!

Some of the m
fun, memorab
and inspiring
days with
Sir Richard
Branson BTS
our cover shoo

Celebrating being a proud
ambassador for
@sydneydogsandcatshome

For 70 years they have offered
a safe haven for thousands of
lost, abandoned and mistreated
animals. Grateful to spread the
message far and wide.

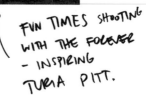

FUN TIMES SHOOTING
WITH THE FOREVER
- INSPIRING
TURIA PITT.

Kick. Start. Smart conference launch. This was such a milestone for us in living the *Collective Hub* Why: igniting human potential!

Gorgeous morning with Heidi Klum.

Hanging with Jack Dorsey, co-founder of Twitter and Square.

The launch of the Graduate Certificate in Collective Entrepreneurship with Torrens University. A dream of mine to disrupt education!

Issue #35 – The Sir Richard Branson cover shoot on Makepeace Island.

Learning to surf with Steph Gilmore.

FRESH NEW OFFICE IN SURRY HILLS! HELLO BIGGER TEAM AND EVEN BIGGER DREAMS!

2017

National Achievers Congress in Melbourne following Gary Vaynerchuk. Public speaking was once my most feared thing. These days I'm on a stage on average 2–3 times a week. Love sharing my learnings with you x

INTERVIEWING JASON SILVA

Collective Hub x Wellness. Bringing yoga to our office dec[k]

WE OPEN THE DOORS TO CO-WORK

Cover interview with Jamie Oliver.

When I started Collective Hub I made a cover-star bucket list:
1. ~~Sir Richard Branson~~
2. ~~Jamie Oliver~~
3. ~~Martha Stewart~~
4. Oprah Winfrey – only 1 more to go!!

Synchronicity and Serendipity

When you connect deeply with your Why, the most extraordinary opportunities appear, seemingly out of thin air. The synchronicity and the serendipity and the people who believe in you when you step into your Why are off-the-charts *insane*!

On the previous pages, I've included a small sample of what my journey has looked like over the last four years, since I stepped into my Why.

I never imagined I'd ever have the opportunity to sit down, one-on-one, with Sir Richard Branson – on his own private oasis, Necker Island. I never imagined to then go on to co-chair a Virgin Panel on 'Smart Disruption' alongside him.

I never imagined I'd pick up the phone one day and John Cleese would be on the other end of the line (seriously!) – a mutual friend had given him copies of the magazine and he wanted to tell me how much he liked it. He was incredibly humble, intelligent and funny. I still find the entire experience surreal.

I never once imagined that I'd get the chance to interview game-changers like Martha Stewart or Ewan McGregor – *Collective Hub* was one of only two media outlets in Australia that Ewan spoke with at the time. Add to that list Jamie Oliver – we were the only Australian media outlet to secure him for a cover on his tour here in May 2017. In between, we've connected with Arianna Huffington, Iris Apfel, Jack Dorsey, Drew Barrymore, Sophia Amoruso and so many other amazing game changers, thought leaders, rule breakers and style makers who resonated with our Why and chose *Collective Hub* to share their stories.

I never imagined that I'd be approached by Disney to be a princess, as part of a campaign showcasing a different kind of role model... or that they'd approach me a second time in one year to be an ambassador for *Beauty and the Beast*.

I never imagined that I'd sign a deal with Simon & Schuster in New York City after being courted by four different publishers... that I'd be picked up by the best literary agent in the United States, seven years after he rejected me.

I never imagined I'd have the opportunity to speak into so many lives, to support hundreds and thousands of courageous entrepreneurs in the *Collective Hub* community, and champion them on along their journey.

I never imagined I'd be surrounded by a community who believes in my Why as much as I do, who come to hear me speak and buy my books and allow me into their lives.

This list could go on and on!

I realise in this book I haven't personally talked a lot about giving back as part of your Why. It's actually the main crux of my book *Money & Mindfulness* and an incredibly important concept to me. In this new book, I've opened it up so you can hear first-hand from some inspirational friends, how giving back is intrinsically linked to their personal Whys. However, I do want to add one thing. In my experience, when your Why is bigger than you or has an impact that is way beyond self-serving, the synchronicity and the serendipity just seem to fall into place.

You Don't Have to Go Big

If I could only choose one word to describe my life over the last four years, my word would be 'Big'. Capital B Big. That's the only way I can even begin to summarise it – my days have been crazy, chaotic, incredible, exhausting, exhilarating, packed-to-the-brim… and that's the quieter days!

That's not to say you need to choose a big life, too. Whether you choose to do something that places you in the public eye or something that sees you operating in the background, it doesn't matter. It's the *choosing* and *committing* part of the process that puts you right in your grace zone and allows the most incredible things to manifest in your life.

HOW TO ASK THE UNIVERSE FOR WHAT YOU WANT

I am *very* specific, conscious of and intentional about my language around pretty much everything. I believe that the words we speak give clear indications of where we're at, and the reality we create for ourselves. If I'm carrying out some habit that I don't want to continue, I always talk about it in the past tense to draw a clear and definite line in the sand around it being an old behavioural pattern.

I am *never* vague about anything – I actually wrote a lot about this in *Money & Mindfulness*. I get very, very specific with my desires and then I completely surrender to them. It's not: "I want to travel." It's: "'I want to spend six weeks in London on a paid work exchange or fellowship," or "I want to go on a girls' week to Bali within the next 12 months."

I work hard to have a clear, uncluttered mind – free of negativity – so that it's a clean channel from which to send forth desires. I use practices such as meditation, yoga, tai chi and qigong to help with this.

I do a lot of vision boarding. It's not enough to just write it down. To truly see your vision come to life, you have to create a visual representation of what that life will look like.

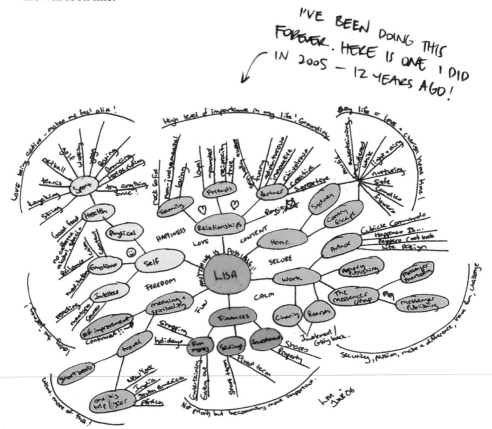

WHAT HAPPENS IF YOU DON'T GET
WHAT YOU WANT?

Accept that it's just not
the right time...

Look for the lesson...

Take note...

Park it for later...

And surrender to the Universe,
knowing that your time will come.

*The power in me is
bigger than any situation
I am facing in the world.*

– JAN BOMMEREZ

WORD FROM THE WHYS: GABRIELLE BERNSTEIN

Loud and proud.

As a 'spirit junkie', spiritual entrepreneur and and #1 *New York Times* best-selling author, Gabrielle Bernstein is the poster girl for living your Why – with grace and passion. After featuring in *Collective Hub*, she also contributed a beautiful meditation for my book *Money & Mindfulness*. Now, Gabrielle shares her three-step process for living your Why loud and proud:

ONE

Understand your fear. I have learnt to become the witness to my fear-based thoughts. Each time I felt fear set in, I'd take a deep breath, step outside of my thoughts and actions, and witness my behaviour. By witnessing my fears, I was able to see how delusional they actually were. For instance, early in my career when I ran a public relations business, I *hated* negotiating my fee. It made me feel anxious and jittery, and I'd lose my sense of calm. When I acknowledged my fears around negotiating for more money, I realised it was related to a belief I'd picked up that women shouldn't ask for more. This was an outside projection the world had created – and I'd chosen to believe it. When I got honest about my fear, I was able to see how this 'lack' mentality had become a fear-based pattern in my mind.

TWO

Be willing to change. The slightest willingness is all you need to receive the guidance to change. When we become open to let go of our fear, we open our hearts, minds and energy to be guided to a new perspective. Willingness raises your consciousness of new possibilities and ignites what I call your ~ing (your inner guide). Your ~ing is the voice of love, your inspiration and your intuition. All you need is a little willingness to get your ~ing on and receive guidance to change. This guidance will come in different forms: intuition, inspiration and synchronicities. Inspiration can be experienced as a feeling of flow and excitement, which comes through in moments when our thoughts and actions are aligned with love.

THREE

Practise gratitude. An emphasis on living a grateful life creates more abundance, acceptance and appreciation. In order to transform your fears back to love, you must embrace a way of being that puts gratitude first. The more you choose gratitude, along with forgiveness and love, the more miracles you experience. If you're wondering what I mean by 'miracle', I'm referring to that shift in perspective from fear to love. A miracle can be the moment you choose to forgive your ex-lover and let go of decades of resentment; the moment you recognise that losing your job was not a tragedy but an opportunity to follow your true calling. Each moment you choose love over fear is a miracle – and when you choose to perceive love over fear, life begins to flow.

living a grateful life creates more abundance, acceptance and appreciation

– GABRIELLE BERNSTEIN

WHATEVER YOUR WHY, MAKE SURE YOU LIVE IT

Life is short.

Seriously short.

Seriously!

Don't let it pass you by.

Don't let anything stop you from being
the *best* version of you.

Take chances.

Don't be afraid of risk.

Or regret lost opportunities...

You only live once and it can be gone in an instant –
so make each day truly count.

And when you finally get your Why,
don't let your calling pass you by for fear of family or money.

All we have today is now, so live in the present.

YOU are in control of your destiny!

Keep Grounded
In Your Why

When I was writing my first book, *Happiness Is...* I learnt something really interesting. I went around Australia asking people what made them happy – about 300 of them, in fact – and while their responses were mixed, they mostly consisted of surface-level answers that reflected society's expectations: "walking on the beach"; "spending time with family" etc.

This reaction was what I expected. It was fine... it was safe. But it was the second reaction that truly surprised me – and at times threw me a little – because people got mad.

When they were asked such a simple, yet loaded question, some people got defensive and cranky. Because they realised they had never really thought about it... Or, they *had* thought about it but they were living a life so far from their ideal, core Why, that they found even discussing the subject of happiness confronting.

I get it. I've been in that place before. But the only way to overcome it is to dive straight into the hard places, where you really don't want to go, so you can come out the other side with a richer, more joyful, purpose-led life.

What I've learnt from years of doing personal development, and becoming a massive queen of manifesting my Why, is that it's best to get really, really specific.

Someone recently said to me, "I have many loves."

Sensing his openness, I pushed a little and asked him to list those loves.

"Travel, yoga, family, friends, food," he rattled off.

I pushed a bit further and asked, "How do they make you feel?"

At this point, the conversation changes. It gets trickier to answer once we drill down to this level, because it becomes about expression and feeling, and with that comes a level of vulnerability.

My friend answered: "Travel makes me feel free. It immerses me in other cultures. I like to learn about different ways of life."

Good. Let's keep going.

Now we've immersed ourselves deeply, three levels in. Let's dare to go a fourth.

Whatever your love is, try to ground yourself in a specific feeling. A specific moment. So you can capture it and really understand it.

How did you feel: free, uninhibited, messy, unshackled? Or perhaps you thrive in ordered chaos: did it make you feel whole, supported, loved, complete?

Recall your most treasured moment and drill down to the specific details. Feel it, deeply, so you can replicate it, return to it and draw strength from it when everything seems too hard.

This is why the simple things in life are often the best. The moments. Because we can capture them, feel them and replicate them, again and again.

... bliss

... being there. Being useful. Happiness is friends and family. Listening to mentally active and dedicated people. Happiness is space and quietitude. The birds singing, the frogs croaking, Looking beyond the hill. Being warm in winter.

... discovering wild places and wild creatures. Nothing inspires or delights me more than the natural wonders of this world. I cannot go back in time to see what was but I can go to the edge of the world to see what is. I believe balance is a myth, so I will climb any mountain, brave any desert and cross any ocean if it means connecting with the astonishing and beautiful creatures who share our planet. I have it on good authority that the priceless elixir of eternal youth can be created naturally simply by staring into the eyes of a curious tiger or inhaling the breath of a Tasmanian forest. After such an experience you may stop smiling when you are asleep, though I can't be certain.

... love of my family.
... my son and his ... with strength.
... happiness. My ... to the fullness ... I, I am happy. I smile, I am ... , I am bold, I am strong.
Be true and just be.

... having a fantastic past and looking forward to an even better future!

Andrew

... of jigglers and
... always see the
... full, never half
... en taking tea at
...osa Main Beach.

... sharing moments of joy and fun with loved ones and friends.

... being able to wear my hair naturally

... gazing adoringly into the mirror and seeing ... w truly fabulous I am

... being able to wear REAL FAKE FUR

... ou're lucky enough ... ny best girlfriends

... cosmetics abuse

... tox, and Paralox

... WHATEVER!

HERE ARE SOME PAGES FROM MY FIRST - EVER BOOK : HAPPINESS IS ...

ACKNOWLEDGMENTS

Every single day from having the idea in my head to now, has brought a smile to my face! I thank the universe every day for the momentum this book has gathered, the synchronicity, serendipity and such incredible support from so many people. Thank you to all of you who believed in my vision so strongly and worked so hard to make it happen. Without a doubt, this has been one of the most fun, happy times of my life. So without further ado, thank you to everyone involved in this book but especially...

... going to mummy's w... Playing with my fri... school. Spending tim... my dog

... learning, practicing and being proud of our culture.

YOU MAY NOT KNOW
YOUR WHY NOW.
YOU MIGHT NOT KNOW
IT 10 YEARS FROM NOW.

BUT REMEMBER,
ONE DAY IT WILL CRYSTALLISE
AND YOU WILL LEARN
THAT YOU'VE HAD IT
ALL ALONG.

WHEN TO WALK AWAY

A huge part of this journey is about knowing when to listen to your ego and *when* to ignore it – while also knowing your boundaries and staying aligned to your Why.

When I launched *Collective Hub*, I wanted to unearth the story behind the story, to be aspirational and inspirational, and to avoid being trashy, superficial or too surface level.

Once you start having some success and brand awareness, people come at you with opportunities that are lucrative – and they can be really hard to turn down. This is why it's essential to be completely rooted to your Why, so you can call on that commitment and focus when you're tempted to stray, or when an ill-fitting opportunity knocks that seems far too good to pass up.

In year three of the *Collective Hub* journey, I was wooed by a well-known TV production company, offering me a very, very lucrative TV deal. Our talks – and there were several of them, over a long period of time – were going really well.

They seemed to understand my vision and purpose for the *Collective Hub* community, which is all about igniting human potential and living your best life. The aim of the show was to go with people around the world and support them as they do crazy things – all in the name of stretching themselves to grow and change and step into the very best version of themselves. Tick, tick, tick... I was excited!

The TV production company and I were on the same page and the project was gaining some serious momentum. Until... they dropped the bomb. They wanted a plastic surgeon involved in the concept. Turns out, we weren't on the same page at all – like, not even a little bit.

Don't get me wrong, I'm sure plastic surgery has its place. BUT I wanted to demonstrate that there are so many powerful ways to transform your life from the inside out by putting in the work. Our message at *Collective Hub* is all about authenticity, realness, embracing your flaws and putting in the hard yards, rather than looking for quick fixes. So, you can see why a plastic surgeon didn't feel like a good fit for us – at all.

Our conversations ended there. Literally, I walked away from what would have been a very profitable and lucrative contract. Ultimately, it didn't align with my values or my Why, so it failed my litmus test.

Still, I know that a TV show is on the cards for *Collective Hub* – in fact, it could be happening sooner than you think. And when it does, I'll be proud to say that I waited until the time and Why was right.

COLLABORATE CONSCIOUSLY

Does your Why align with the people you collaborate with? It doesn't have to be an exact fit – hopefully your offering is unique – but there are some key aspects that should match. What is their ethos, their vision, their work ethic? Is their goal to make money or to find meaning? Do they truly care about their customers and their employees?

It's not rude to delve into these topics when you first meet a possible collaborator. In fact, it's essential if you don't want to be distracted from your Why by a negative influence. I LOVE collaborating – it lifts me up, energises me and inspires me. But, a word of warning: be careful about who you invite into your creative sphere.

WORD FROM THE WHYS:
LORNA JANE CLARKSON

I've known my beautiful friend Lorna Jane for many, many years, since we began collaborating on her first best-selling book. She was our inaugural cover star on *Collective Hub* magazine and she shares many of my beliefs around purpose and Why. So, while writing this book, it seemed only fitting to approach Lorna to share some of her thoughts. As the founder of an activewear label, Lorna Jane, that inspires women the world over to live their best and healthiest life, Lorna absolutely and unequivocally lives her Why. Here are her thoughts on getting to the root of your most important question: *Why do you do what you do?*

"Why is a question I constantly ask myself, not just in business but also in life, because I truly believe that understanding the purpose behind why you are doing something is just as important as understanding what you are doing.

"My Why is simple, and it's been the same since day one – to inspire women to live their lives with purpose and passion. I believe to do this you need to take care of yourself, and that's what my Active Living Philosophy and the daily practice of 'Move Nourish Believe' is all about. It's the very thing that makes me bound out of bed in the morning, the thing that I can't go a day or even an hour without thinking about, the thing that I believe in with all of my heart... It's my purpose, and I honestly believe it's the reason for my existence.

"Life is full of choices, and they're not always easy ones. But, every single decision I make as a designer, an author, a mentor, a boss, a wife, a sister, a daughter or a friend comes back to this Why. Understanding your Why changes everything and it makes what you are doing so much more meaningful.

"I may have huge goals and dream bigger than big, but at the end of the day I'm just one person trying to make a difference in the world, one woman at a time. I don't want to just live a life, I want to leave a legacy, and that's my purpose. It's what keeps me going when I've been working for 12 hours straight, it's what inspires me on those days when I'm not feeling motivated, and it's something I couldn't imagine not being part of my life.

"I think you find your purpose when your passion becomes something you chase every day. I didn't set out with the intention to build a global brand – it happened because my Why was, and still is, the biggest motivator in my life. I think the success of the Lorna Jane brand is true testament to what can happen to you when you're honestly and sincerely living your purpose."

I think you find your purpose when your passion becomes something you chase every day

– LORNA JANE CLARKSON

IF YOU'RE STUCK, ASK YOURSELF
THREE SIMPLE THINGS:

ONE

If money was no object,
what would I spend my days doing?

TWO

What was I doing the last time
I completely lost track of time?

THREE

How would I like to spend my
last day on Earth?

IF THE ANSWERS AREN'T EVEN CLOSE
TO HOW YOU SPEND YOUR TIME NOW,
THEN YOU DESERVE MORE.

Let your passion point
be your guiding point
in every decision
you make.

Who Am I to *Not* Keep Going?

Here's the truth: in 2016 I almost gave it all away. Everything. The magazine, the brand, the business, the lot.

My discontent started seeping in slowly, and when I finally reflected back on it, I could see what the problem was. I was stepping away from my Why, rather than stepping into it.

Where I thrive is in the middle of the chaos: I love big-picture planning and strategy, problem-solving, coming up with ideas and solutions, and sinking into the creative.

Where I don't thrive is in the detail. In 2016 I found myself mired in – I was up to my eyeballs in staffing details, magazine details, HR details, financial details and operational grind… It was detail overload, and I didn't cope with it well, at all.

To compound things, as I got busier and busier last year, I found that I let my self-care go. My routines and rituals, which are so grounding and so important to me, were sliding. I knew what my non-negotiables were. However, they were starting to fall by the wayside because I was struggling to keep my head above water, let alone remember to meditate in the middle of a stressful day.

This meant that when the sh*t hit the fan – which it did, in spectacular fashion – I didn't have my usual support infrastructure to turn to.

So I did something drastic. I packed a bag and fled to India in October 2016. When I arrived, I was emotionally hungry and desperate. I'd got myself into such a risky position with the business, which was on a downwards spiral, and I was making massive personal sacrifices – health, relationships, friends, family, everything – along the way.

That journey to India turned out to be transformational in more ways than I can explain. It changed my life (again!) and forced me to turn inwards, while also flipping every belief I had on its head to analyse what was truly going on back home.

After the retreat – 11 days of going deep, being completely removed from all technology, digital connection and external noise – I felt renewed. When I returned to Australia, I dug deep and found reserves of energy that I didn't even know existed! For 12 weeks I went full throttle – with a renewed toolkit that kept me safe and nurtured, and enabled me to go hard and fast again without completely burning out. And I turned every aspect of my life around. Business? Tick. Beautiful new relationship? Tick. More grounded, present family time? Tick.

I've experienced monumental life shifts like this before when I've chosen to invest time (and money) into reconnecting to my Why. The experience was so transformative that, and this probably won't surprise you, I've been madly writing the basis of yet another book, which will detail exactly how I got so far down the rabbit hole, and how I pulled myself back out again.

In 2017 life is very different for me, which is why I chose to return to India in a renewed frame of mind. This time, I'm faced with a different conundrum. Life is good. Really good. And now, life is *so* good that it's about setting intention to move, grow, expand and unleash on an entirely new level.

Here's the thing that I know for sure at this point: I'm 16 years into the business and four-and-a-half years into *Collective Hub*...and I still don't have it all figured out. Not by a long shot. It is still a daily imperative for me to learn, expand, push myself and get uncomfortable. I believe massively in the power of continuous improvement, continuous checking-in and challenging ourselves.

STUFF COMES AT US
ALL DAY
EVERY DAY

THAT WE CAN'T CONTROL.
WHAT WE CAN CONTROL
IS HOW WE RESPOND
TO IT.

As you know by now, I'm a whole-hearted advocate of getting comfortable with being uncomfortable.

After going through the highs and the serious lows of 2016, what I know from the core of my being, and what I have talked about incessantly across every conceivable platform since launching *Collective Hub*, is that your Why is an absolute imperative.

It's the thing that drives you every single day, the thing that keeps you going when you feel like you are at your absolute limits and in the depths of despair. It's the one thing that has the power to propel you forwards, to shock you into action, and to drag you out of bed when every single fibre of your being just wants to crawl back under the covers and give in.

Throughout the last few years, my deep connection to my purpose has helped me to navigate the dark times of running a business. This journey has been so much harder than I ever anticipated. If I had known back then what it involved, would I still do it? Yes! Again and again!

Once You've Found Your Why... How Do You Stay on Track?

Surround yourself with people who support you.

———

Never get complacent about what you're doing.

———

Put yourself back in your greatness zone.
Things that weaken you? Ditch 'em.

Continue to make the choice to be part of the solution in the world, big or small.

———

Be really prepared for what happens next. Sometimes, when people suddenly find some sense of success or celebrity, they turn into narcissistic arseholes. Don't let that happen to you!

What to Do When You Feel Like It's Slipping Away

This starts to happen to all of us at some point. None of us are immune to it, for a variety of reasons.

Here's what I've learnt: success can be a scary thing. It can also be completely overwhelming. The thing is, when you step into your purpose, suddenly an absolute avalanche of opportunities start coming your way. And so it's easy – *really* easy – to grab at everything and start doing way too much, spreading yourself way too thin – to not have the skillset or, even more worryingly, the mindset, to keep you grounded and propel you to the next level.

So, heed my words from experience. This advice is imperative, and sometimes the hardest thing to do. Ready? When everything is good and smooth sailing, use this time wisely to gear up on the tools that will stabilise your mindset for the times that are unexpected.

I have fallen victim to this more times than I wish to share (but I'm sharing with you anyway, it's part of my Why!). When it's great – when your career is swimming along beautifully, you have loads of energy and you have a great partner – you feel like you are untouchable and you can take on the world. In this space, it's easy to get complacent and even a little arrogant.

But, trust me, the Universe has ways of reminding us that we are not invincible. I believe if we are genuinely seeking and open to learning, the Universe will put difficult, unexpected times in our path – in order to propel us to the next level, to become the very best version of who we are meant to be.

This has happened twice to me in big, unexpected ways over the past four years, since starting *Collective Hub*. Both were unanticipated and both could have absolutely knocked me to my knees and paralysed me, had I not had a bank of skills and tools at the ready from years of business and personal experience, and self-development.

The first was a horrible, heart-wrenching break-up two years into the *Collective Hub* journey, when I had been at an absolute all-time high in every aspect of my life. It was the best time and I felt on top on the world – so much so that I wrote a book professing my happiness, called *Life & Love*. Just weeks after releasing the book, I received what felt like the smackdown of the century when my partner left.

Only, it wasn't. Because as horrifically hard as that time was, even through it, I was able to be grateful and to say: "Wow – I really did not see that coming. Thank you, Universe – this is truly a test for me to see if I can handle this with dignity and grace, and move through it and forwards."

The second was four years into the *Collective Hub* journey. We had experienced such rapid growth and with that came a need for some serious systems, processes, operational procedures and a lot of detail. I started working much more 'in' the business than 'on' it and started to completely lose myself… We were on a pretty rapid downhill spiral and I could have lost everything.

Thankfully, though, because my Why was so inextricably linked to every cell in my body, I had the tools, awareness and consciousness to recognise the potentially tumultuous mess I was about to put us in. And I enabled myself to get still and quiet (hello, India), reflect on my Why and get back to putting people in place who were the 'yin' to my 'yang' – the detailed, operationally focused people who would quickly complement my weaknesses and support me in systemising my vision and making us run effectively and efficiently once again. If I didn't know Why I did what I did in those heart-wrenching moments, there is absolutely *no* way we would have made it through. *Collective Hub* would not be here today. GULP… If that's not a reason to really step into your Why, I don't know what is!

Train yourself to be you best on your worst day

I cannot begin to tell you how proud I am now that I did move through both those experiences with dignity, humility and grace. And because of that, I honestly feel I now deserve a place to really live my purpose and help other people to ignite their own potential.

Here's the kicker: if I hadn't personally been through so many hard times and periods of adversity, how could I truly choose a purpose of helping others to live their Why? From what platform would I be speaking? How could I empathise with people, genuinely and authentically, if I hadn't truly lived the highs and lows?

SEE! Even at the toughest point in my journey, I could check-in with my Why and make sense of the struggle. I could check-in with my Why and find purpose in my pain. I could check-in with my Why and know that even these horrific experiences, the dark days and heartbreak, were only helping me to achieve my mission.

For this, I am thankful.

Your Why will become your best friend, your greatest mentor, your shoulder to cry on, your reason for smiling, the constant in your life that supports you, shelters you and inspires you, even when other circumstances change around you. Your Why is so much more than a mission statement – it's a map for you to follow, which will lead you to the light and out of the shadows.

Your Why is wise.

It's yours.

It's waiting to be found.

And once you've discovered it, you'll wonder where it's been all your life.

You've got this!

Be clear.
Be decisive.
Take action.
That's it.
No more, no less.
Just do.

TED Talks

THE POWER OF PURPOSE
Steve Taylor

"With a strong sense of purpose, we can push through obstacles, we can transcend any obstacle."

"Purpose gives us resistance to negative psychological states like depression, frustration, anxiety and boredom."

HOW TO FIND AND DO WORK YOU LOVE
Scott Dinsmore

"I wanted to find the work that I couldn't not do."

WHY SOME OF US HAVE DON'T HAVE ONE TRUE CALLING
Emilie Wapnick

"Embracing your inner wiring leads to a happier, more authentic life."

BEFORE I DIE I WANT TO…
Candy Chang

"Making a space for reflection and contemplation and remembering what really matters close to us as we grow and change."

STOP SEARCHING FOR YOUR PASSION
Terri Trespicio

"If you sit around waiting for passion to show up and take you there, you're going to be waiting a long time. So don't wait. Instead, spend your time and attention solving your favourite problems."

"Don't wait, just start doing."

TO FIND WORK YOU LOVE, DON'T FOLLOW YOUR PASSION
Benjamin Todd

"Do what's valuable. By this I mean focus on getting good at something that genuinely helps others and makes the world a better place. That's the secret to a fulfilling career."

HOW TO KNOW YOUR LIFE PURPOSE IN 5 MINUTES
Adam Leipzig

"Each of them knew something about their life purpose because they knew five things. Who they were, what they did, what they did it for, what those people needed or wanted, what they got out of it and how they changed as a result."

2005 STANFORD COMMENCEMENT ADDRESS
Steve Jobs

"I'm convinced that the only thing that kept me going is that I loved what I did. You've got to find what you love."

BY THE WAY, THIS ONE ISN'T A TED TALK BUT I JUST HAD TO SNEAK IT IN. AS IT'S SO GOOD!

TV Series and Documentaries

FINDING JOE (2011)

Conversations with everyone from Deepak Chopra to Tony Hawk and Rashida Jones, about the hero's journey and how we pursue our individual and/or collective sense of purpose.

MAN ON WIRE (2008)

Philippe Petit, French tightrope walker, hire-wire walks between World Trade Centers, a poignant portrait of what one person is capable of.

PROJECT HAPPINESS (2011)

Four students explore the world to better understand the universally desired notion of 'lasting happiness', and how we all have the potential to be happy if we are open to change.

THE KING OF KONG: A FISTFUL OF QUARTERS (2007)

Two men compete for the title of World Champion on Nintendo's 1981 arcade game, Donkey Kong – unexpectedly dramatic, engaging and inquisitive, about finding purpose in the strangest of places.

JIRO DREAMS OF SUSHI (2011)

Jiro Ono, a three-Michelin-star 87-year-old sushi chef, finds a way to disrupt an age-old tradition and has dedicated every day of his life towards his passion.

PLANET EARTH (2006–)

Fascinating forms of beauty within our natural world, narrated by the one-and-only Sir David Attenborough, who has the ability to put everything into perspective.

HALF THE SKY (2012)

Eva Mendes, Olivia Wilde and America Ferrera are just some of the familiar faces telling the stories of lionhearted women who are bringing awareness to women's oppression worldwide.

PARKS AND RECREATION (2009–15)

Leslie Knope's unwavering optimism is infectious as she aspires to help the people of Pawnee, one community project at a time. Charming comedy, with unique endearing characters.

THIS IS US (2016–)

Characters who are trying to figure out who they are in the world. Easily relatable, heart-warming.

CHEF'S TABLE (2015–)

Original to Netflix, documents some of the most renowned chefs in the world. Each episode takes viewers on a journey into the life and kitchen of the chef, as they share their story and unwavering passion for their craft. Truly inspiring.

IRIS (2014)

A gawk into the excessively accessorised world of 95-year-old Iris Apfel – a New York City stalwart who is as eccentric as she is iconic. Comes care of famed documentary filmmaker Albert Maysle. This one will get fashionistas frothing at the mouth and many more will be inspired by Iris's words of wisdom, pithily delivered from behind her signature specs.

MAIDENTRIP (2013)

What were you up to at 14 years of age? Dutch youngster Laura Dekker was setting out on a two-year voyage in pursuit of becoming the youngest person ever to sail around the world – having fought a 10-month court battle to be able to make that trip on her lonesome. Inspiring? Oh yeah.

Movies All About Why

Into the Wild (2007)

The Secret Life of Walter Mitty (2013)

Good Will Hunting (1997)

Doctor Strange (2016)

Trainspotting (1996)

Million Dollar Baby (2004)

Hidden Figures (2016)

Milk (2008)

Cinderella Man (2005)

Forrest Gump (1994)

Wild (2014)

Whiplash (2014)

The Motorcycle Diaries (2004)

Dances with Wolves (1990)

Erin Brockovich (2000)

Podcasts

ON BEING WITH KRISTA TIPPETT

Interviews with scientists, theologians, artists and teachers exploring life's most meaningful questions. Weekly hour-long segments bound to teach you something new about your existence.

THE MOTH

TED-style talks but from everyday people who are funny, informative and even heart breaking. Insights into how regular, relatable people are finding their sense of purpose and what we can learn about being human.

TED RADIO HOUR

Get your TED fix on the go with the podcast version of their renowned series of thought-provoking, purpose-building, problem-solving talks.

BENJAMEN WALKER'S THEORY OF EVERYTHING

This podcast begs you to really question what's going on in the world and the role you ultimately play in it. Connecting the dots between art, culture, media and tech, 'Theory of Everything' makes you think big picture.

BULLETPROOF RADIO

Advice on building the very best version of yourself physically, mentally and emotionally, so you can be unstoppable, mindful and bulletproof.

MINDSET ZONE

Leave your old view of the world behind and prepare for a growth mindset, in terms of you, your purpose and your future.

LONGFORM

Interviews with non-fiction writers about how they find purpose in their work, create their own style of storytelling and their modus operandi.

THE DAILY BOOST

Skip your regular coffee run and get your daily dose of energy from these bite-sized chunks of motivation – sharing advice on minimising stress, maximising happiness and mastering life skills.

THE MINIMALISTS

The two experts on how to live a meaningful life with less. Their message is a simple one: re-evaluate all the stuff in your life and only keep things that bring you joy.

GOOD LIFE PROJECT

Inspirational, unfiltered conversations with big names in the biz, but also ordinary people, on how they found their sense of meaning, purpose, spirituality and success in life.

TINY LEAPS, BIG CHANGES

Rather than simply spouting out vague-yet-catchy sayings about purpose, this podcast offers tiny steps to inch you closer towards your big overall change. Practical ways to make progress on your journey towards a life of purpose and passion.

About The Author

Lisa Messenger is the vibrant, game-changing founder and CEO of *Collective Hub*. She launched *Collective Hub* as a print magazine in 2013 with no experience in an industry that people said was either dead or dying. *Collective Hub* has since grown into an international multimedia business and lifestyle platform with multiple verticals across print, digital, events and, more recently, co-working spaces – all of which serve to ignite human potential.

Lisa is an international speaker, best-selling author, and an authority on disruption in both the corporate sector and the start-up scene. Lisa's experience in publishing has seen her produce over 400 custom-published books for companies and individuals as well as having authored and co-authored 24 herself. Most notably, Lisa charted her ride to success with her best-selling book *Daring & Disruptive: Unleashing the Entrepreneur* and its sequels *Life & Love: Creating the Dream*, which reached #1 on Booktopia; *Money & Mindfulness: Living in Abundance*, that shot to best-selling status within the first month; and *Breakups & Breakthroughs: Turning an Ending Into a New Beginning* soon followed.

Her passion is to challenge individuals and corporations to get out of their comfort zones, find their purpose, change the way they think, and to prove there is more than one way to do anything. She encourages creativity, innovation, an entrepreneurial spirit and lives life to the absolute max. Most mornings she wakes up and pinches herself at how incredible her life is, but is also acutely aware and honest about life's bumps and tumbles along the way.

With fans including Sir Richard Branson, *New York Times* best-selling author Bradley Trevor Grieve, and a social media following of over 150,000, Lisa's vision is to build a community of like-minded people who want to change the world.

In between being a serial entrepreneur and avid traveller, she loves nothing more than being at home with her dog, Benny, gardening and collecting as many indoor plants as humanly possible.

Acknowledgments

TO MY WONDERFUL, INSPIRING AND TENACIOUS COLLECTIVE HUB TEAM:

Thank you to my team – every single one of you, past and present, who have created and worked tirelessly on this dream. You are like family and I will be forever grateful for your selflessness, loyalty and love for what we have and are creating with *Collective Hub*. There will be tough times and highs and lows, but having you all by my side every day makes the purpose and vision unwavering and unshakable. Knowing we have a combined purpose and a Why and are working together to achieve that is the greatest reason to get up every day. Here's to a big, bright and beautiful future for us and our incredible community. Sarah M, Jen, Amy M, Claire, Georgia, Ash, Soph, Jas, Emily, Tara, April, Joz, Nicole, Bridget, Whitney and Lisa D – thank you from the bottom of my heart, the depths of my soul, and every cell in my body.

TO THE PEOPLE IN MY LIFE WHO MAKE EVERYTHING BETTER:

To my family that forever keeps me grounded, to my superstar personal assistant, Georgia, who is by my side every day complementing all the bits that really aren't my sweet spot. And, of course, to all my amazing, wonderful friends who make life full of colour.

TO THE ONES LIVING THEIR WHY OUT LOUD

To the thought leaders, change makers and rule breakers living their Why out loud and proud – the ones who inspire me every day without even knowing it. To our *Collective Hub* community, this book is for you.

Speaking Opportunities

Lisa is available for speaking opportunities. Her key message is 'Anything is possible'.

Her keynotes are highly engaging, energetic and really get audiences raring to face, and overcome, any new challenges head on. Using self-deprecating humour and colourful anecdotes you'll hardly believe, Lisa will take your audience on an incredible journey.

Some of her speaking topics include:

Cultivating a killer self-belief

Finding passion and purpose

Creating an amazing team culture

Failing fast

Strategic partnerships

Thinking big and going global

Challenging your personal limits and overall thinking

Building a personal brand or business

Disrupting in business and within a corporate

Developing a sixth sense

Investing in yourself

FOR MORE INFORMATION, BOOKINGS AND BULK BOOK SALES
ENQUIRIES, EMAIL BOOKINGS@COLLECTIVEHUB.COM
OR PHONE +61 2 9699 7216

Collective Hub

Collective Hub launched in 2013 as a print magazine in 37 countries, and quickly became a global sensation.

Today, it has evolved into a true international multimedia business and lifestyle platform that encompasses engaging digital content, bespoke events, strategic collaborations and unique product extensions.

Across it all, *Collective Hub*'s vision and purpose is to ignite human potential. Everything we produce exists to inspire and educate people on how to become the best versions of themselves so that no human potential goes wasted.

Combining style and substance with a fresh perspective on the issues that matter most, Collective Hub covers business, design, technology, social change, fashion, travel, food, film and art.

Whether you are looking for a boost of creativity, professional advice from industry experts or a warm and practical pep talk, *Collective Hub* is your go-to guide to making an impact in the world. It's a place where people share their aspirational stories to inspire the next wave of change makers.

We are insatiably curious, naturally collaborative and uniquely creative. *Collective Hub* inspires entrepreneurial thinking by empowering our community to live their best lives at work and in play. We offer pragmatism and inspiration in equal measure to help create a world of dreamers and doers.

COLLECTIVEHUB.COM

@LISAMESSENGER #LISAMESSENGER
@COLLECTIVEHUB #COLLECTIVEHUB

Other books by Lisa

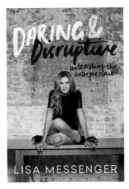

AVAILABLE AT SELECTED NEWSAGENTS, BOOKSTORES, TRAVEL
+ AIRPORT STORES OR VISIT COLLECTIVEHUB.COM

Your Vision

Created by Collective Hub

BESPOKE CONTENT CREATION
WHAT YOU MAY NOT KNOW ABOUT US:

Before the launch of *Collective Hub*, The Messenger Group was (and remains) a celebrated marketing agency with more than a decade's experience in branding, public relations, content creation, community management and marketing. We assist our trusted partners in creating a band of loyal consumers and a more cohesive brand identity through content creation and custom book publishing. Previous clients include Lorna Jane, Pollenizer, Ninefold, CBA, Toby's Estate Coffee and PwC.

WHAT WE CAN DO FOR YOU:

Combining our expertise in branding, public relations, content creation, community management and marketing, we are specialists in delivering the stories our clients want to tell. By tapping into the power of captivating content, we can assist in encouraging a two-way conversation between company and consumer.

HOW WE CAN HELP:

By designing and creating content for a variety of:

- Print media (books, journals, diaries, magazines)
- Digital media

TO FIND OUT MORE, EMAIL US:
CUSTOMPUBLISHING@COLLECTIVEHUB.COM

COLLECTIVE HUB 101
MASTERCLASS
—

LAUNCH THAT BUSINESS. LAND THAT DREAM JOB. GROW YOUR BRAND.

PRESENTING
COLLECTIVE101

– a series of **masterclasses** taught at *Collective Hub* HQ in conjunction with a unique line-up of entrepreneurial pioneers who will educate and equip you with the skills and knowledge to ignite your career or business.

SIGN UP NOW AT

COLLECTIVEHUB.COM/COLLECTIVE101

PURPOSE